Oɴᴇ Sᴇʀᴍoɴ ᴀ Yᴇᴀʀ

D1528339

One Sermon a Year

Selections from Two Decades in the Pulpit

The Reverend Donald K. Campbell, II

Donald K. Campbell, II
510 Brookside Drive, Apt. 32
Little Rock, Arkansas 72205
501.219.6846
revdcampbe@aristotle.net

ISBN: 978-0-9972312-3-6

Book and cover design: H. K. Stewart

ask
BOOKS
P.O. Box 251301
Little Rock, AR 72225

Printed in the United States of America

This book is printed on archival-quality paper that meets requirements
of the American National Standard for Information Sciences,
Permanence of Paper, Printed Library Materials, ANSI Z39.48-1984.

FOR MY GRANDCHILDREN

Table of Contents

Letter to My Grandchildren

Dear Aaron, Paulina, Catherine, Celeste, Grace and Andrew:

Some years ago, realizing you have known me only as an old man, I wrote my memoirs to record what my earlier life was like. Volumes I and II have been published. Volumes III and IV, telling of my years as a minister, have been written but won't be published for some years because of confidentiality issues. I doubt they would be of interest, anyway, until you are middle-age or later. That's when people get curious about their heritage (so they can pass it on to their grandchildren) and by then the people who could talk to you about it will have passed on.

As I was writing in Volume III about my nineteen years as a pastor I remembered I had boxes of old sermons. The Butler Center for Arkansas Studies wants them as evidence of what was being preached in Arkansas during the 1950s and 1960s, the civil rights era and the Vietnam War. Before turning loose of these I decided to pick out one sermon from each of those nineteen years to give you as a sample of what I was thinking and saying. If you are going to be middle-aged before reading memoirs, you'll probably be ancient before you read sermons! But these are offered to you if you ever do get curious.

Of all the aspects of the parish ministry, preaching was the one I liked least and felt was my weakest skill. I usually put off sermon writing until Saturday night or into early Sunday morning. I was not a "popular" preacher. But as I read these over I do believe I took seriously the Bible passages for that Sunday, and usually had something to say. However, you can judge for yourself, if you ever read one or more.

There are some caveats before you start:

- The sexist language is terrible! I was tempted to "correct" it, but that's the way people talked and wrote in those days. I did not become sensitive to sexist language issues until 1974, after I moved to Atlanta.

- In 1998 a fire in my apartment destroyed all the sermons from 1954 and 1956, so I included two from 1955 and two from 1957.

- Sermons in those days were much longer than people would tolerate in 2016. But I still think "sermonettes are given by preacherettes and make Christianettes."

- If you read these you might want to skip the first few (and come back later) because I think my preaching improved as I gained experience.

- I did not start using sermon titles until about 1965 when one member said a title in the bulletin would aid him in remembering what I'd said—and might even help him understand while I was saying it. To help you decide which sermons you might read and which you know you'll want to skip, I've gone ahead and added titles to all of the sermons in this book, even if they didn't have one when I preached them.

- Some of these sermons were included because they referred to events important in the life of our family.

- As I plowed through these documents I was struck by illustrations taken from current events that brought to mind crises that had faded from my memory. They are little "snippets" from the history of that time.

- In one sermon I commented I was sure there were issues not yet on our horizon that would surface in the future. Feminism, drugs, gender identity, relations with other world religions, and the decline of mainline religions had not really become major concerns.

If you ever read these you'll find out what was going on in your grandfather's mind 1954-1973 when I was pastor of two small Presbyterian Churches in the State of Arkansas. They are part of your heritage, whether you like it or not.

Love,
Grandfather
December 2016

The Presbyterian Church of Crossett

Crossett, Arkansas

GOD CORRECTS OUR CONDITION

Date: January 16, 1955—Second Sunday after Epiphany

Lectionary: Psalm 27; **Isaiah 41:2-13**, 17-18; **St. John 2:1-11**

Hymns: "Glorious Things Of Thee Are Spoken," "The King Of
   Love My Shepherd Is," "We Give Thee But Thine Own"

*I had been pastor in Crossett less than three months, only since
November 1954.*

Have you ever noticed how often in the Bible the Word which
comes from God is the opposite of, the corrective to, the prevailing mood of the people to whom it is addressed? This is one of
the reasons why it is almost essential to learn something about the
historical background of any book in the Bible before you can really
get the most out of what it has to say. For instance, in the story
about the wedding feast at Cana of Galilee which I read this morning, there is a flurry of consternation within the household over
the shortage of drink for a feast—on the part of the servants, on
the part of Jesus' mother, and there would have been humiliation
for the bridegroom had the wine run out. And into this situation
Jesus stepped with the needed corrective of a new supply of wine.

But when in place of sorrow men had calm self-assurance our
Lord did not speak words of comfort. Instead, he proclaimed judgment which laid a man's soul bare. A rich young ruler came to ask
the way toward eternal life—confident that he had already found

and fulfilled that way. To such self-righteousness Jesus said, sell all that you have and give to the poor, and come and follow me. And the man was sad, as he turned away, for the weakness of his soul had been bared. In face of such assurance there was no word of comfort.

Throughout the Old Testament we find demonstrated the same kind of corrective to our human excesses. Some of you children, not long ago, studied about how Kind David was a mighty man. Once, when he had been weak he depended upon God, but in his power he no longer relied on the Lord and did as he pleased. Then the Word of God came to him through the prophet Nathan. He told how a rich man with many flocks and herds, spying the one little ewe lamb of a poor man, took it. When David was shocked by such sinful use of power Nathan pointed a finger at him and said, "You are the Man," and the smallness of this mighty king was revealed. And when, at a later time, the rulers of Israel were wealthy and could afford to lie on ivory couches because they were exploiting the poor and buying the needy for the price of a pair of shoes— when these things were happening God sent one of the sternest of his prophets, Amos, to speak to them His Word. And Amos' message was a series of "woes." Among other things he told them that people who put their wealth and might to their own use would be the first taken off into exile. To people satisfied with their own comforts God sends a word of warning and judgment.

The earlier prophets had brought to the haughty Israelites messages of doom. Now, when the doom is about to overcome the faith and hope of Israel, comes another prophet with a different message. People felt that Babylon was so powerful that it would rule the world forever, just as we assume western democracies will be the controlling force in the world, at least for many years. But the prophet points with confidence to "one from the east" whom he later identifies as Cyrus, a Persian. He assures the despairing Jews that this Cyrus will break the yoke of Babylon, placed about their necks, and free them from the Babylonians and the Greeks as this victor from Persia approaches. They have been relying on idols and gods which they have made by their hands out of wood and metal to protect them. These false gods obviously could not help Babylon in her hour of need and the prophet laughs as he watches the people nailing them down and soldering them together so that they cannot be moved. The empire of Babylon is soon to collapse and the Jews freed to return to Mt. Zion. This is part of the comfort which the prophet brings to a captive people when he sings:

> Comfort, comfort my people,
>   Says your God.
> Speak tenderly to Jerusalem,
>   And cry to her
> That her warfare is ended … (Isaiah 40:1-2)

But the prophet speaks much more; else he would have nothing to say to us. It matters little to us that empire of Babylon has collapsed, for so has the one of Persia. But it does matter a great deal to us that God is the Lord over the great movements of history, and that He takes them and uses them for his own purpose of teaching and saving His People. The prophet assures Israel that Babylon did not conquer Jerusalem because Babylon's gods were more powerful than Israel's. Nor does Persia's power lie in her gods-for actually, none of these gods exists at all. There is only One God, and He controls the fate of all nations. He allowed Jerusalem to be taken because the Jews were haughty. He now allows them to return from Babylon because they have been brought low.

Our prophet tells us more about God than just that He has might enough to control the destiny of nations. He is also a God of tenderness. He is moved with pity at the plight of His people. To Israel he says: fear not, be not dismayed; I will strengthen you, uphold you, I will help you. When Israel is brought low and is on the brink of despair He calls them by endearing names: "Jacob, whom I have chosen," "the offspring of Abraham, my friend." When the Israelites are described as people lost in a desert where "…the poor and needy seek water, but there is none…I the Lord will answer them…I will make the wilderness a pool of water." When His people were proud God brought them low. Now that they have been humiliated and know that they are nothing, God comes to them with comfort and healing and strength to raise them up.

We are very fond of these passages of comfort—"Comfort, comfort my people, says your God…(and) fear not, for I am with you, be not dismayed, for I am your God." But are these meant for us as a group—as a nation, as the organized Church, in a day when we are riding the crest of the wave? These words were addressed to a defeated nation, an exiled religion. Does God promise to maintain the United States as the world's greatest power; or has He committed Himself to keeping the Church a booming business in America as it now is? No. The word which has come through all the prophets is that God is Lord over history, and His greatness did not depend upon Israel's sovereignty nor does it rest upon America's might. Nations rise and nations fall, and our belief is that God works for good in all these changes. If the mighty nation rests in the confidence of its own power, then it is for its good to be brought low. The real strength of God's people does not rest in number of members or the richness of their buildings. Church historians predict that as the human strength of the Church has moved from Europe to America, so in the future the financial and intellectual centers will be in Africa and Asia, the mission fields of today. And if this comes true, if the Church in the United States loses its vogue and many of its numbers, it does not mean that our God has lost His strength. It will be the humbling word which is always spoken to the mighty; and when we are brought low then we will be able to accept the assurances of comfort and strength without thinking of ourselves as the source.

But while we as a nation, or as a multiplying church, hardly seem fit for promises made to exiles; as individuals we are often in great need of them. Singly we rise and fall rapidly—from day to day and hour to hour. There are times when we seek comfort from God, and comfort is not the word He has for us, but rather judgment because our vanity and our self-confidence persist. If we turn to these passages of comfort primarily as a means of escaping the word of judgment we will find in them only the printed word, and not the living Word of God. But if we turn to them because we have already been brought to see there is no power in ourselves, if we turn to them because we know that the only living hope is in God-then we are ripe to hear His assurances, and He will come to us as Living Water for one whose tongue is parched with thirst. The prophet of the Exile knew that God remains God however bad life seems at the moment; and he also knew that He has an extraordinary tenderness for His little ones who are lost and needy. These assurances are the comforts intended for those who have been brought low. They may have little to say to you at the moment if you and your church and nation are all surging ahead in self-confidence. But if you have been brought low, or when in the future you learn what it is to be one of the weak and rejected of men—then you have the sure knowledge that God waits to lift up His fallen ones, and comfort the sorrowing.

Parental Love for Two Brats

Date: July 3, 1955—Fourth Sunday after Trinity

Lectionary: Psalm 20; Acts 3:11-21; **St. Luke 15:11-32**

Hymns: "Love Divine," "Depth Of Mercy, Can There Be,"
    "Show Pity Lord, O Lord Forgive"

When Dr. George Buttrick, now chaplain of Harvard University, arrived in Little Rock he was questioned by the reporters concerning the alleged revival in this country. When asked if he thought such a rebirth of Christian life was going on Dr. Buttrick replied, "There is no revival where there is no repentance. I do not see signs of widespread repentance in our nation." And what he said is what every true preacher of Jesus Christ's message has said since the time of the first apostles, because repentance is an integral part of any real relationship between a pure, yet loving, God and sinful men. We read this morning from the Book of Acts one of St. Peter's early sermons and we find the same theme there: "Repent therefore, and turn again, that your sins may be blotted out, that times of refreshing may come from the presence of the Lord." Re-pent means literally, re-think. The necessity of such re-thinking and changing of our ways is illustrated as well as anywhere in all literature in the story we read this morning from St. Luke's Gospel, the one we normally call the Parable of the Prodigal Son. Actually, it should be called the parable of the one loving father and the two prodigal sons. For we have drawn for us three personalities in the brief story—the Father, about whom I shall speak in a few minutes; the younger son who was a prodigal or wanderer because he was unrighteous; and the old brother, also a prodigal, not because unrighteous but self-righteous. We do not normally speak of him as a prodigal, but in fact he was. He was no more in relationship with his father than was the younger brother off in a far country living riotously.

We are told in the story that this young man came to his father, asking for that part of the inheritance which would be his. We get the impression from talk of servants and rings and robes that the father was a wealthy man—and certainly this is the impression Jesus wanted to convey. The share which would go to the younger when there were only two sons in a family was one third. This would be a large amount of money he would have. We are not told exactly what he did with it except that he wasted it on "loose living," and the elder brother bitterly resents one who has wasted money on women of ill-repute. It's not hard to imagine just what did take place—it has been repeated ever since this story was first told, a life devoted to passing pleasures, always looking for a new thrill satiating one sense and being driven on to more dangerous escapades in order to get any kick. It looks like fun from a distance as long as the music is playing, the parties last all night, and the money flows freely. For the poor wretch caught on this merry-go-round and unable to get off it is often in sheer hell even while the calliope plays and the horses go up and down. When the ride is over and there are no more nickels to pay the owner the gay party boy is run off into the shadows and all the world can see how miserable he is. How many of these men end up on skid-row and the women spend their days in fifth rate hotels. The only notice the world gives them is scorn, and not even that when men can keep them out of sight. This is the picture presented of the younger brother who went off into a far country. Jesus wanted his hearers to grasp just how down and out he was. As you know, the Jews consider pork unclean, and hogs the lowest of all beasts. As a mat-

ter of fact, they even refused to name the name of hogs and referred to them as "the other thing." Jesus said this boy was to the
point of spending his days tending the unmentionable animals, and
even envying them the food they ate. He has sunk to the absolute
bottom because of his unrighteous living.

We are told in the story of a second brother. He was not unrighteous. Far from it. He was a hard worker, we gather, for he was
still in the field when the feast began. He reminded his father that
all these years he had remained at home, doing whatever his father
commanded. We get the picture of a man who wants to know just
what is expected of him in order that he may not do less—or more;
of one who wants to know precisely what others expect of him, and
what he in return may ask of them. We have etched for us the por-
trait of a man who is correct, always; but one from whom the last
drop of love and mercy and kindness has been squeezed. He has
wasted no money; he probably never got drunk in his life. When
someone says to him "repent, therefore, and turn again, that your
sins may be blotted out" he probably looked around to see who the
culprit was. How can one repent when he has lived a clean, decent
life? Jesus was surrounded by people who reacted to calls for repentance in just that way. They were called Pharisees. You and I are
surrounded, in the Church, by many elder brothers who speak of
repentance with a gleam in their eyes, remembering the young boy
now living in a far country. A New Testament scholar, asked one
time if he knew who the elder brother was replied, "Yes, I discovered
his identity only yesterday—myself." Some of us here are younger
brothers who have begun the long trip back from the far country.
Probably most of us are like the elder son. Dorothy Sayers has divided all sins into warm sins and cold ones. Most of ours are on the
cool side—jealousy, greed, laziness; setting ourselves up as God, ignoring the needs and joys of others. And because they are cool they
don't smell so much, and we often forget they are there. A call for
repentance comes and we wonder who's been caught.

We are shown rather clearly the kind of men these two sons
were. What happened to them? It is easy to overlook but interesting

to note that we are never told for sure what happens to the elder brother. I had always assumed that he remained like he had been, that he kept his two thirds of the property, but was never restored to a relationship with his father. That certainly is the implication of the parable. His last words show him still bitter, isolated, self-righteous. But his words are not the last ones in the story. These are the father's gracious offer of love and forgiveness, expressed concerning the wanderer come home. Certainly they were also meant for the elder brother too, if he could come out of his shell of legal purity and receive them. But the story really doesn't conclude at all—it has an open end. You have the feeling that there is still a chance for this brother if he will take it. Most of us hope he will. Do we still choose this way for him when we see ourselves as elder brothers who wonder what talk of repentance has to do with us?

And what happened to the younger brother? We know a good bit more about this. After he reached the very bottom of life, in the far country, he came to himself. Literally, he did repent, re-think. He realized that he had sinned. He resolves to confess, to accept any punishment resulting from his choices, and go once more to his father. The elder brother could of course have done the same thing, but he didn't. Sometimes I wonder if people aren't fortunate when their sins are the lurid, socially disapproved ones. I don't mean to make light of the havoc they play with lives. Reckless driving isn't just something to joke about when you hear of selfishness on the highway taking the life of some young person, or sending another through life with a misshapen arm. Loose living, sexually, does tremendous damage to those who find life existing only when going from one thrill to the next; and the hurt is deeper still on those whose family life is weakened by deceit and divided loyalty. No, I couldn't make light of the sins of the flesh after being on mental hospital wards filled with the frames of people whose minds have been destroyed by syphilis. Nor would I make light of the disasters which can come through alcohol. When a woman neglects her children during their early years because she doesn't have complete control of herself, nothing she can do at a later time will erase the damage she has done to their personalities. A home broken because of alcoholism often cannot be restored even if sobriety is regained, for in the meantime one or both partners have remarried. No, these so called "warm" sins are terrible in their consequences. But I sometimes wonder if they do not have more seeds of hope buried in them than the cold ones of greed and pride. They are so obvious that they sometimes bring people to face their utter defeat and absolute bankruptcy so that they are more willing to repent and turn again than those who have sinned more respectably. Last Sunday we went to an open meeting of Alcoholics Anonymous at the Cummings Prison Farm. A man stood up before his fellows and began by confessing that he was completely defeated, that he could do nothing apart from God. A man whose sins place him behind bars has strong reminders of his need. Life with the swine served the same purpose for the younger brother. At any rate, he turned and headed home, seeking help from him whom he has wronged. The call for repentance is the call for each of us to do the same, whether we begin our homeward trip from feeding swine or behind bars, or from the field where we have been working, full of self-righteousness.

But the younger brother did not head back home to an empty house. He returned because waiting for him was the kind of person whom Jesus has depicted in the father. Had he not already known at least something of the loving nature of his father he would never have gone back. And this is true for all of us. Unless we are at least partially convinced that God is merciful you and I will never choose to make our confessions. A great many so-called Christians conceive of God only as a stern police-court judge, meting out punishments and rewards. If I have sinned and that is what He is like, of course I'm not going to return to him. I might just as well stay in my pigsty. The younger son knew enough of mercy to begin his homeward journey. But while we have to have some knowledge of God's love to repent, it is never until we have made our full confession that we have anything like a full grasp of how deep that love is. And again, the younger son found this to be so. He knew his father loved, so he determined to return. He expected at the most from his father to be protected and fed as a servant. Instead he found that the father's love restored him as a son.

Many of us object to such love as weak and sentimental, and encouraging people to sin. We object to this picture of God as indicating that He doesn't take sin seriously. Surely the father suffered deeply from the sins of his son-the loss of his property was real; the years of separation when the son was living with harlots could not be restored; the knowledge that his son had lived with swine would forever hurt a Jewish father. And so does God, our Father, suffer over our sins. His offer to forgive does not mean that our playing loose with the lives of others, our bitterness of heart, our making ourselves God in His place is of no consequence. Forgiveness does not mean that God shuts His eyes. Forgiveness comes when God is fully aware of all we have done, when he absorbs into Himself the pain of our insults to Him and to others, but still loves and wants to take us back. The good news which Jesus came to tell was that God is like the father who said, "It was fitting to make merry and be glad, for this your brother was dead, and is alive; he was lost, and is found." The requirement to hear these joyous words is that we repent and return to the father, whether it be from a far country or from a respectable field just beyond the house.

This is what Jesus came to tell us God is like, if we'll just admit we need him, repent and return home, and let him restore us as His children.

Don't You Believe It!

Date: August 25, 1957—10th Sunday after Trinity

Lectionary: Psalm 40; **Acts 9:1-9**; St. Matthew 6:1-15

Hymns: "Praise Ye the Lord, The Almighty," "Prayer Is the Soul's Sincere Desire," "Sometimes a Light Surprises"

As a result of a June 17, 1998 fire in my apartment the notebooks containing all my sermons from August, 1955 through March, 1957 were destroyed. Since there is no evidence of how my preaching may have developed in 1956 I am including two sermons from 1957.

*D*on't you believe it! The church spends a lot of time teaching us what we ought to believe, but it also has a few things to say about what we should not believe. One of the things it rules out is the assumption that what has been will be for ever and ever; the belief that major changes cannot be made in the way people think or feel or act, in the structure of society or in the corruption that may riddle a government. The Church does not shut its eyes to the reality of handicaps or the power of sin. But it knows from experience that human life is not a sealed unit like an electric light bulb, from which no gas can escape and into which none can enter. God always has the right of access into a man's life—and God is powerful, powerful enough to bring about changes and create revolutions.

This is something that some of us need to hear again, to hear until we finally believe it in place of the worldly maxim that it's foolish to hope for any major changes. This is not abstract theology I'm talking about. It's the way you live. You have someone in your family who is emotionally immature and unable to live up to the responsibilities which are thrust on him because of his position. There is one you love who is physically ill and the doctors know of nothing they can do for him. You have personality problems of your own that were given to you by your parents as a little child and now they have grown to the point of making you useless to yourself and a pain in the neck to others. You are caught in a job situation which is destructive to your moral values and is slowly remolding you into the image of something you have always despised—yet you have a family who must eat, and you can see no way out. Have you ever known any one of these situations—these traps which seem to be escape proof? Then you have known what it is like to live in hell. But the Good News of the Gospel is that we are not doomed to remain just as we are without hope. For life is not hermetically sealed against God. There is the possibility of His entering, and where He enters there are opportunities of deep and revolutionary change.

There's no way to prove this. All one can do is to tell the story of people to whom it has happened and offer you the assurance that the same thing can happen to you.

It took place in a part of the world which was pictured on a map on the front page of the *Gazette* one day this week. A boy was born in the southern part of Turkey in a university town not far inland from the Mediterranean Sea. His family apparently was fairly well to do with a number of important connections. They were also deeply religious, belonging to a very strict denomination—and they drilled in him the belief that anyone who didn't live up to all the rules was damned and even more than that, that such a person would be a source of temptation to others and should be put out of the way. In order to see that he was given all the opportunities—for he was a very bright boy—the parents sent him while he was quite young to be educated by the denomination's leading teacher who lived in a city several hundred miles away. There the young man apparently did very well for he was taken into the inner circle while he was much younger than most of his colleagues, was even put on the governing body. But there was one thing that he didn't learn. His teacher was a man with a very big heart, who was willing to let people differ with him at least until he was absolutely sure that they were not right. The young man from Turkey however absorbed none of this. He must have been warped before he left home. He was the kind who had everything all lined up and organized. It was very clear in his mind what should be thought and done, and all who disagreed with him were wrong and should be blotted out. People like this are obnoxious enough when they are not being challenged, but when someone dares to hold onto and spread some new ideas they just go into a frenzy. They become wild, saying things they don't mean, doing things they will regret later. Perhaps you have known someone like this. We're inclined to despair of them.

Well, this is what the young man from Turkey got like when his pattern of life was challenged by a group of people who claimed to know a better Way of life, the Way of Jesus called the Christ. He stood by assisting when they killed the first of these followers of The Way. As I said, he had been put on the governing body by now, the Sanhedrin, and he voted to have a lot more of them killed. Then, in order that none should escape, he got a warrant for the arrest of those who had fled from Jerusalem to the city of Damascus. This is the same Damascus about which we've been reading in the papers, the capital of Syria, the country that may be slipping behind the Iron Curtain. By the old road it's one hundred thirty six miles from Jerusalem to Damascus. That's eight miles less than the trip from here to Little Rock. They didn't have cars in those days, and the scholars say that by the old road it would have been a six day walk. You can imagine the state Saul was in—for that was the young man's name—as he got within the last few miles of the hiding place of these people who he thought were damned and trying to corrupt others. He must have been tired after the long trip, and most of us are at our worst at the end of a journey. He had been with a group of men under his command for six days—and doubtless they spent much of the time telling themselves how right they were and how wicked were these people who followed Jesus, the man who had been put to death by the government. Unfortunately we are also familiar in our own day with hate groups—people who gather together for the one purpose of hating another group, be they Jews or Japanese or Negroes or capitalists. They egg each other until they become almost crazy with hate. Saul had been with his hate group for six days, and the victims were almost within their grasp. The Scripture says he was "breathing threats and murder." It was the atmosphere in which he ate and slept and breathed. He was not some stupid lout who had had his emotions played on by a clever leader. He was educated, he was intelligent. He knew what he was doing and was convinced it was the right thing. If ever there was a person who we would have thought could not be changed it was Saul of Tarsus, as he drew near to Damascus.

Then the unexpected happened. A light from heaven, brighter than the noonday sun! A noise which others heard but could not understand—a noise which for Saul was words in the Hebrew tongue, spoken by the same Jesus whose followers he was seeking. When Saul rose he was blind and had to be led into the city. There he remained in solitude and darkness for three days. When the third day was over a change had been made. Saul was approached by a man whom he had been sent to capture. Instead of seizing him, Saul welcomed him, went to the place where those who followed The Way were gathered, was baptized and even preached in public that this Jesus whom he had scorned was the Son of God.

Don't you believe it! No, it's not the story you're to disbelieve. It's the assumption that people can't be changed, even people who have thought through their positions or those who have been molded that way from childhood. People can be changed because God can enter life. They can grow, they can mellow, they can reverse direction. There is no one too far gone for God to work with.

Let me tell you another story. It doesn't go back quite so far. Ten years ago I was in a political science course at Yale. A few rows in front of me sat a boy who was the personification of Ivy League sophistication. He was so wealthy and socially prominent that he could wear his father's clothes that were twenty-five years old, or appear in clothes that were almost rags. You know, when people rise from poverty to a good income they want to dress well, but when they pass from plenty of money to extreme wealth they often get so they don't really care what people think. The boy's name was Kelly, and Kelly was one of these. His grandfather had been a leather baron in the nineteenth century and his father had never had to work. Kelly was charming and could be polite when he wanted to. But he yawned during the professor's lectures. He wasn't interested in political science. He wasn't interested in anything, really, except Kelly. He hardly knew who God was, for his parents had seldom been inside a church since the day he was baptized. They hadn't even bothered with this for his younger sister. When he was in prep school in California he had been to church once a year, for annually the whole student body came down on horseback to the nearest church and attended in riding clothes. But that was all. Kelly wasn't interested in God, because he didn't know Him. He wasn't concerned about other people except when he found them interesting. He was headed toward a well-heeled life of self-centered boredom. If I had been a betting man I would have wagered my bottom dollar that Kelly was one who could not be changed.

But this summer Kelly took a boat trip. It was a long journey for it was from California all the way to Singapore in Asia where his wife and two children will join him. He is going to a city which may be taken over by Communists any time. He is going to work with people whose color would have barred them from the circles he once knew, who are poorer than his mother's maid would have dreamed possible. He is going to teach Old Testament in a seminary for Malayans who are going to be ministers.

There was no blinding light for Kelly, no voice which made others tremble. It all began when Kelley was asked, hopefully but without expecting "yes" for an answer, to arrange the kick-off dinner for the student charity drive. There he met a few of the

Christians on campus and one or two of the ministers on the faculty. Then he decided, for kicks, he would go to church one Sunday. He was impressed. One day he appeared at daily chapel service, which only a handful attended. He looked awkward as he got down on his knees to pray, and every hymn was a new one to him, even "Holy, Holy, Holy" for he had not sung hymns before. He entered seminary the same fall I did, and the Bible courses were exciting for him because he had never read so much as a chapter of Scripture until a few months before he came to Divinity School. One day the professor said "Turn to Numbers four." Kelly asked, "Numbers what?" Then with the passage of months Kelly grew in depth and breadth. Now he has forsaken all that money and education and social prestige can buy to go to a remote corner of the world to teach people about whom he once had only heard. Don't you believe it! Don't let anyone tell you people can't be changed. I know one who was.

You do too, probably. Do you have any Christian friends who once were willing to mortgage their souls for a dollar, until they had their standards changed? Do you know a member of A.A. who was a slave to drink until Christ through the agency of some fellow-sufferers lifted him up and out of a ditch and started him walking in another direction? Don't you know someone who was an old bear, who didn't have a kind word to say for man or beast, who has been liberated from the need to growl and is now capable of having friends? Surely you know someone who has been changed-and the same possibility is open for you or one you love since God has said He can and will enter lives to make them new.

Don't spend your time and energy worrying about the mechanics of how a change, a conversion, takes place. It never comes the same way twice—just as no two people have identical finger prints. Occasionally it will be a spectacular thing like what happened to Saul of Tarsus on the road to Damascus, with a shining light that can be seen, and a voice that human ears can hear if not understood. More often, it will be silently, secretly. Don't be disappointed if this is the way you get turned around, or your friend.

Jesus said that we ought to try to keep the fact secret if we can, just in the results do we proclaim it to the world. The same variety exists in terms of speed. It may be that God will act with sudden power in reversing your direction; more likely, it may take place over a period of months or even years. But these details are of no importance. The main point is this—the good news that no one of us is caught in such a web of sin or weakness or circumstances that God is not able to break through it and lift us into freedom. We may bear the scars forever, but we can be set in the open and given the chance to walk again. I know some of you are saying to yourself, "but my plight is too great. I am the one person even God can't help." Don't you believe it! God can act, and God will act in those who let him. Have hope and cheer as you pray for him to come quickly.

Holding Leaders Accountable

Date: September 8, 1957—12th Sunday after Trinity

Lectionary: Psalm 51; **Ezekiel 34:1-16**; **St. Matthew 7:1-4**

Hymns: "The Lord's My Shepherd," "Sometimes A Light
Surprises," "Once To Every Man and Nation." The anthem,
following the offertory at the close of the service, was "A
Prayer for Liberty" by Means ("O Eternal God, through whose
mighty power our fathers won their liberties of old; Grant, we
beseech thee, that we and all the people of this land may have
grace to maintain these liberties in righteousness and peace;
through Jesus Christ our Lord. Amen.")

*A sermon preached by the Reverend Donald K. Campbell, II the Sunday
following the action of Governor Orval Faubus in calling out the
National Guard to stop the integration of Central High School in Little
Rock, Arkansas.*

"Judge not, that you be not judged" said Jesus, and then he
turned right around and told His disciples that they would
have to judge. That's what he did when he commanded them not
to cast pearls before swine or give holy things to dogs. He was using
a figure of speech to say that they should not expose the holy truths
of God to ridicule by offering them to people who are not interested
or who are incapable of receiving them. And this calls for judgment-
the disciples had to judge between the interested and disinterested,

the capable and incapable. Was Jesus contradicting Himself? No, because the Greek word for judge has several meanings. One of them is to condemn. Another means to make a moral appraisal. All of us need to be warned to steer clear of the first, censorious judgment; many of us need to be pushed into the second, making moral appraisals. It is so easy to pretend humility and say that we are not qualified to judge on this or that issue. Perhaps we are not perfectly qualified, but we are commanded to distinguish to the best of our ability between right and wrong, between love and hate, between service and selfishness. Jesus did not call us to moral neutrality. To take his words "judge not" and to twist them into that is ethical escapism. It is not permitted for a disciple.

All of life is based on moral appraisal. Every time a banker makes a loan he has to judge the honesty and business skill of the man who borrows. Those of us who have a little savings account at the bank depend on his using his judgment when he lends out our money. Every time a girl agrees to marry a man she should say "yes" only after judging his honesty, his unselfishness, his dependability. When you have a problem which you just have to share with someone, you judge that some of your friends can't keep a secret, and others are incapable of entering into another's problems, until finally you find one whom you judge to be a good listener or confidant. This does not mean we condemn eternally those who fall short. We simply note their deficiencies and decline to entrust them with something too precious for them to handle. We do not cast pearls before swine.

One area in which this art of appraisal must be exercised is the political. We have got to look at our political leaders with open eyes in a bright light to see if they are fit to be entrusted with the destiny of our nation, our state, our county or city. No man would turn over a manufacturing plant to a manager without checking into his abilities and his morals. No farmer would commit the care of a flock of sheep to a shepherd without knowing him well—and continuing from time to time to check up on him. The prophet Ezekiel in our First Lesson this morning likened the leaders of a nation to shep-

herds, because in both cases the ones who follow are so terribly dependent upon them for an abundant life. Sheep count on their
shepherds to strengthen the weak, to heal the sick, to find the crippled and to bring back those who have strayed. In our human society we count on our leaders to provide some of the same helps and
also others-equality before the law, justice in the courts, a fair
chance to earn a living, dignity in the eyes of society, a rule by law
and not by force. But what we expect does not always materialize,
because sometimes the leaders are not really interested in their
flocks, or part of their flocks-they are more concerned about their
own comfort and wealth and political advancement. So the Lord
God spoke by His prophet Ezekiel, "Ho, shepherds of Israel who
have been feeding yourselves! Should not shepherds feed the sheep?
You eat the fat, you clothe yourselves with the wool, you slaughter
the fatlings, but you do not feed the sheep... Behold, I am against
the shepherds; and I will require my sheep at their hand, and put a
stop to their feeding the sheep..." This was not just theory either.
The leaders of Israel had bartered their souls for money, they had
lowered the moral level by compromise with standards other than
those of God, they had betrayed their people through political ex-
pediency and unholy alliances. They were no longer fit to be leaders; God was using Ezekiel as His instrument to speak the judgment,
the appraisal of their behavior. He was carrying out His judgment
by letting Jerusalem be taken captive because of her sins, and her
people be carried into captivity in Babylon.

But the failure of political leaders to be wise shepherds of the
people did not cease with the fall of Jerusalem in Old Testament
days. The kings of France cared nothing for the misery of their people and drained them of money without the slightest concern.
They dared to live in the splendor of the palace of Versailles while
the people rioted for bread. Therefore the king of France was
judged to be an unfaithful shepherd in the protests of the French
Revolution. The bishops of Rome in the 1500s were morally de-
based and cared nothing for giving the people the Bread of Life,
Jesus Christ, nor for teaching them His ethical principles. The bish-

ops of Rome were judged to fall short, and the instrument God chose was the Protestant Reformation. In political democracy God does not need to use violence; and He speaks His judgment not through the solitary prophet like Ezekiel or Luther, nor through the single revolutionary such as Robespierre in France. He rather chooses to have judgment made by countless ordinary folk like you and me—judgment in the sense of appraisal. Judgment in terms of condemnation He reserves solely for Himself—that is none of our concern. But appraisal is—and when the shepherd shows himself unworthy, the instruments of democracy for removing him from the flock are the free expression of opinion, the writing of letters, the casting of ballots, and the running for office. And this is our moral obligation, to do these things.

You and I, as citizens of Arkansas, have in the past week been thrown all of a sudden into a crisis situation where the leader of the flock has been taking some very strong action. We are a rather slow and sleepy state, usually, and don't expect the dramatic to happen here. Some of us never thought it could. But in these six days we have had an experience not unlike that of the English no-bleman, the Earl of Derby, who dreamed one day that he was mak-ing a speech in the House of Lords and woke up to find that he was! We can't believe that it's real-that these things are actually happening in our midst. It's a shock to say the least. Perhaps we're more like the housewife from Cameron, Louisiana who told of her experiences in the Hurricane Audrey. She was caught in the flood-waters and for twenty-four hours floated around, without food and surrounded by snakes, supported only by a bit of wooden wreckage that she caught as it swept past. She said during the whole period she kept thinking this must be just a terrible nightmare—she had read about this happening to others, but it just couldn't happen to her. Yet it did.

And it is happening to us. Our own tragedy is watching the elected leader of our people, for reasons known only to him, take from the people some of the solid values of life which he was en-trusted to make available to all, and offer in exchange the tawdry values of prejudice and provincial loyalty which a noisy group find satisfying for the moment but which none will find lasting in the presence of God. As we all know by now, the Governor of the state called out the National Guard on the pretext of preserving the peace on the night before Central High School in Little Rock was to be integrated according to a plan drawn up by the School Board and approved by the court, and stopped the long awaited change. He did this in the face of a Federal Court injunction forbidding any interference. By so doing he is depriving the people of at least three values of the abundant life. First, he is attempting to deny equality to that fourth of our people whose skins are black; and to at least some of us is denying the cherished privilege of fellowship with a larger circle of God's children than our local customs have heretofore permitted. In the light of the New Testament teaching that in Christ Jesus all dividing walls are broken down, this attempt to rebuild barriers that were beginning to sag is definitely a moral question. But the crisis in Little Rock has passed beyond the issues of segregation-or-integration. That really has slipped into the background. Second, the governor's actions are depriving us of respect for the law and for the established methods of interpreting and enforcing the law. By calling out the National Guard he is saying that obedience to the law is required only of those not strong enough to resist it. The inevitable conclusion of his disregarding the courts is the motto "might makes right." And this is a moral question about which we must make a judgment. The third thing that his action will take from us is an ever-widening circle of concern and loyalty and interdependence. No one who accepts the New Testament hope that all things and all peoples on earth will be made one in Christ Jesus can be content with nationalism as the ultimate loyalty. But the nation comes much closer to the fellowship than does the state, or even one section of the country. The governor's action would assert that the claims of local loyalty outweigh the riches of national life organized by a common government and a common constitution. And anytime horizons are narrowed and fellowship is restricted, the action becomes a matter of morality. On every moral issue the Christian is forced to judge. He must be for or he must be against. To say nothing is to endorse. Christ did not call us to moral neutrality.

At this point it is good for us to remember once more that we are not to judge in the sense of condemn. I'm preaching at myself here to a large extent. If there is evil we are to leave the ultimate destiny of the one committing it to *God* to deal with as He sees fit. But if there is evil *we* are called upon to act in a relative way, to diagnose it and to cut it out of the body like a cancer before it spreads and does still greater harm. Nor do we need to tread lightly, in the fear that we may not have any business taking the speck out of another's eye. My friends, this is not another's eye—this action in Little Rock is *our* deed; it is our eye, and as Christ said there's a whole tree-trunk sticking in it. It makes no difference if you say you did not vote for this particular governor; it makes no difference if you say that you do not approve of his actions. They are not just his actions; they are ours, for we are one; they are ours until we have at least let the world know that we have appraised the situation and found that the shepherd is abusing the flock for reasons which we do not now know, and judge his actions wrong. This can be done by letters to the President and the Attorney General, to the Judge and to the Governor himself. This judgment can be expressed in newspaper publicity and the signing of petitions and by talking to key political figures. This is the way in a political democracy we are enabled to make the moral judgments required of us by virtue of being moral men. And this is one hour in which those judgments ought to be made. We are in the eye of the whole civilized world. The people of Asia are waiting to see what we will say and do; the people of Africa, the converts of our missionaries in Congo, are eager to see if the Christianity in this country has anything to say about leaders who do not seek the abundant life for *all* their flock. We are living in an exciting turning point in history. The time of judgment has come, and each one must speak, or by his silence cry assent.

Once to every man and nation comes the moment to decide,
In the strife of truth with falsehood, for the good or evil side;
Some great cause, some new decision, offering each the bloom
*   or blight,*
And the choice goes by forever 'twixt that darkness and that light.

Jesus, the Forgiver

Date: March 16, 1958—Fourth Sunday in Lent

Lectionary: Psalm 32; **Acts 13:26-33a, 38-39**; **St. Mark 2:1-12**

Hymns: "Praise, My Soul, the King of Heaven," "God, Be
   Merciful to Me," "Depth of Mercy! Can There Be"

*Between February 23 and June, 1958 I preached seven sermons on
"The Person and Work of Jesus Christ." This is the fourth of them.*

W e come today to consider the role of Jesus Christ the
   Forgiver. We might have used the term "Savior" or "Redeemer," the words normally employed to describe this aspect of
His work, but their very familiarity tends to obscure their meaning.
We assume we understand them so don't bother to think about
them at length. But the word "forgiver," a little less common, is
yet so plain that none can miss the point. In his sermon in Antioch
St. Paul said, "Let it be known to you therefore, brethren, that
through this man forgiveness of sins is proclaimed to you…" And
in St. Mark's gospel we read how Jesus made the claim of being
able to absolve men of their guilt and pardon their transgressions.
It happened in the story of the paralytic in which the crowds were
so great that this sick man's friends couldn't get him in the door of
the house where Jesus stayed, so they went up on the flat roof,
pulled some of it off, and lowered the man into the room where
Jesus was preaching.

Today we'll concentrate not on the eagerness of the friends, but on the words Jesus first spoke when He healed the sick man. He said at first not "You are well, so get up and walk" but "My son, your sins are forgiven." It's hard for us to understand what the connection between physical paralysis and sin is, because we believe that illnesses are normally caused by germs, and sometimes by psychological quirks. We don't connect my case of flu and your measles with sin. The people of Jesus' day did, however. Some of them had even worked out a system by which they thought they could tell what the sin was by the type of illness which came. Jesus, being a man of His own generation apparently accepted this interpretation of sickness. He assumed that the man tied to his bed must be in need of forgiveness, and therefore He granted it to him.

You and I are not usually made aware of our wretchedness by crippling sickness—though of course this can happen as we have learned in psycho-somatic medicine. Surely the physical collapse of the FCC Commissioner Rich Mack, the man involved in the scandal about the Channel 10 TV station in Miami, was not unconnected with the burden of guilt that he had long carried and the shame that has now come upon him. But normally we stop short of the bed—we instead drag through living at about fifty per cent of capacity. Our fears make us hesitant to try a new job, or meet a new person. Our anxieties make us miserable when we give a talk or write a paper or prepare a meal for company; our hostilities toward people to whom we dare not express them—people like the boss, or the wife—crop out in unexpected places, making us quick and sharp with innocent folk like our children, our neighbors. And because of this we grow lonely. These fears and anxieties and hostilities are to a large extent the result of our sin. We have grown up in a "dog-eat-dog" world where it is the accepted thing for every man, every nation, to look out for his own interests, even if it means shoving someone else aside. This is selfishness, putting one's self first—this in sin. And it makes many of the weaker brethren fearful of venturing forth. Some of us are among this group. We'd like to be freed of fear, and of the sin which causes it.

Some of us are hostile—we have sneers and sarcasm sticking out on us like a porcupine's quills, ready to wound and hurt anyone who comes near us. A lot of our hostility is because of frustration, and the frustration can come from the meaninglessness in life—a lack of a sense of direction. Meaninglessness is a sin for it is the ignoring of One who came to show us the Way, a meaning for life. Some of us need to be cleansed of the crippling burden of hostility, and of the sinfully undirected life which causes it. You and I were not brought to the Lord's house this day on a bed, nor did friends have to make a hole in the roof to let us in. But we are sick—some of us physically, all of us emotionally and spiritually—and if there is a way of being healed we'd like to know about it.

Jesus called His healing "forgiveness"—"My son, your sins are forgiven." What is forgiveness? Is it just forgetting unpleasant things that have taken place? Is it, even worse, knowing that wrongs are there but pretending that they are not, like putting a band-aid over a cancer and call it just a minor infection? Is forgiveness the act of making light of sins that have been committed? No, not at all. True forgiveness can take place only where the one who has sinned and the one who forgives take seriously what has been done. Jesus forgave Zacchaeus, but he regarded the tax collector's cheating gravely enough to expect him to repay four times over all that he had stolen. Jesus forgave the paralytic who was let down through the roof—but he did not say "Let's forget the past and pretend it never happened." Forgiveness looks with open eyes at the wrong done, measures in specific terms the effects that have been, or will be, felt, and then covers it over like a man who puts new shingles on a roof that leaks. Forgiveness acknowledges that we have been captives, then frees us from imprisonment, like the payment of ransom releases a prisoner from the clutches of his kidnapper. Forgiveness cannot restore life to exactly its previous condition, it cannot make things appear as though there never had been any hurt done at all. Forgiveness is like the healing of a wound on your body. It is the growing of new tissue, the closing of a gaping hole torn in the flesh. When you've had a bad wound you may be healed but you bear the marks with you until your dying day. You will always show you were wounded. But you are a *healed* victim. You and I will always show we have been sinners—but we can be healed, or forgiven, sinners. And forgiveness is like the healing of the body in another way. Scar tissue may be ugly but it is often stronger then the original flesh. It's not a pretty thing to have to be forgiven—but the new lease on life granted to the sinner is often grabbed at and lived out more fully than the first stage of life before there was sin. And this is always a part of forgiveness—not just the cancellation of wrongs in the past, but the entering into a new era of life with new sources of strength for the days to come. Jesus said not only "your sins are forgiven" but also "rise, take up your pallet and walk."

Well, how can this forgiveness be given and received? It's important to realize from the first that forgiveness is not a commodity like lumber or paper; nor is it even an idea like the theory of relativity which has value and reality not dependent upon the person who conceived it. Forgiveness is personal, just as sin is—it has to do with the restoring of personal relationships. You cannot sin against a thing—you may abuse a thing but you sin against the one who owns it. So only a person can forgive the wrong—only the one against whom it was committed has the power to renew the fellowship severed by the abuse. Each human being has the ability to forgive, but it limited to only those sins which were committee again him. If you were to drive recklessly and in the midst of your foolishness ran over me and so injured me that the doctors had to amputate my leg—you would have sinned against me, and I would have the opportunity to forgive you. But if you ran over the Methodist minister instead, then the strained relationship would be between you and him, and he only could pardon your transgressions against him. This of course also applies to group actions—we can forgive the Japanese for the treachery of Pearl Harbor, because they acted against us as a nation. We do not have the power to forgive our mass bombings of Tokyo—only those who were deprived of homes and loved ones can offer to heal the wounds caused by that part of the war. But Jesus said to a paralytic who was bought to Him, "My son, your sins are forgiven." So far as I can tell, the sick man had had nothing to do with Jesus. It would seem they probably never met before. How could Jesus offer such a sweeping—such a "blank check"—forgiveness? It could be done only if He was present in all those against whom the paralytic had sinned, regardless of who they might be; only if He had felt the pain of all the wrongs done by this man from the day he was born. No one but Almighty God does this. No one but God knows all the wrongs, experiences all the sins, of the world. No one else has the right and power to make an all-inclusive act of pardon, and the scribes caught this at once. "It is blasphemy! Who can forgive sins but God alone?" They were right. None but God could do it—and therefore Jesus blasphemed, He put Himself in the place of God without cause—or else the alternative must be true, that Jesus of Nazareth is God—God of God, Light of Light, Very God of Very God. The choice is clear when Jesus claims to be the forgiver of the sins of the whole world. Either he is the Son of God—or He is a liar, a cheat and a fraud. I believe that He is the Son of God, and I believe that I can and must go not only to those whom I have consciously wronged to ask for pardon—but I must go to God in Christ as well, for he is wounded by my transgression against them. And when I do not know whom I have abused, when my best efforts to remember cannot recall a full record of my words and deeds, I can go to Jesus Christ alone—for he has experienced all that I have done wrong. He has the right to forgive.

How far will His forgiveness go? Are there not some things which are unpardonable? Jesus does speak at one point about the unforgiveable sin which is sin against the Holy Spirit—but it is very difficult to know what He means there. For all practical purposes, you need never worry about having committed a sin too big for God to cover with His love. In the parable of the prodigal son the young boy goes away and wastes half of his father's wealth and brings grief to his heart—but still there waits for him at home a welcome that is warm and free. If you have committed sins of the flesh, or sins of youthful foolishness, God in Christ will forgive them. When Jesus was nailed to the Cross on Calvary men had done the worst to Him—yet through parched lips and in the midst of agony he said, "Father, forgive them." If you have murdered, if you have abused God, if you have blasphemed, Jesus Christ will forgive you still.

I've told this story before but it bears repeating of a man who was riding on a train one day when he saw a young boy across the aisle obviously upset. He moved over and soon they began to talk. The boy confided that he had run away from home. He wanted to go back. He thought they would take him, but he wasn't sure. His home was on the railroad tracks, so he had written a card saying he would be on a certain train on a certain day. This was it. If they were willing to receive him back and forgive him would they, he had asked, tie a handkerchief to a certain limb on the tree in the front yard? "Mister, we're getting close to my house. I'm afraid to look. I'm going to shut my eyes, and will you look for me?" He described the house and the tree. The train rounded the curve and whipped on by. The boy's eyes opened and fastened on his companion's face, half hopeful, half fearful. The man reached over, took him by the arm and said, "Son, there was a *sheet* tied to *every* limb on that tree."

We need never fear that we have sinned so deeply that He cannot make us clean. Jesus came to make this clear. This is good news for you. Whatever sins, whatever guilt has been troubling you and burdening you—know now that it is forgivable. Come to the Savior, the Redeemer, the Forgiver, and let Him make you well and strong and whole again.

Abide in Me

Date: January 4, 1959—Second Sunday after Christmas,
    Holy Communion

Lectionary: Psalm 91; **I John 4:9-16**; St. Luke 2:21-32

There is no record of the hymns sung.

The sacrament of Holy Communion was celebrated in Crossett on the first Sunday of every month. This was considered very "high church" and out of step with the practice of most Southern Presbyterian congregations that had communion only once a quarter. On this Sunday there was also a baptism.

In our first Scripture lesson this morning, the one from First John, we read of a kind of relationship between man and God which has been offered to you and me. It is described there by the word "abide"—"we abide in him and he in us." This word "abide" itself tells us at least three things about the relationship.

The first is that it is *personal.* I have been able to find in literature only one place where our English word "abide" is used to describe the action of something other than a person, human or divine, and there the subject is the "peace of God," almost inseparable from Himself. In every other instance it is a person who abides, or who is invited to come and dwell. On Easter evening the disciples walking on the road to Emmaus said, "Abide with us, for it is toward evening, and the day is far spent," because they believed their unknown Companion to be a man. When we sing that hymn of longing "Abide with me, fast fall the eventide; the darkness deepens, Lord with me abide" we are not pleading for the support of an idea or a Great Power or a Life Force, but a Person, a Father, One of whom we use the pronoun "he" rather than "it." And this was promised us when we were told that our relationship can be that of abiding together.

In the second place the word "abide" makes clear that our relationship with God is not a temporary, transitory, one, but *endures* across great periods of time. Abide is not a word that we would use when inviting someone to drop by for a quick cup of coffee. Abide means to stay while, to continue in one place, to sojourn or tarry. Actually, "abide" is almost archaic, a word we seldom use any more—and perhaps the reason being that today we jump around like crickets, rarely staying any place for long at a time. But though we may be always on the go in every other area of life, we learn that any relationship with God will abide, remain. It is the eternal God, for whom a thousand years are as one day and one day as a thousand years, who draws near. And when we invite Him to stay with us because the darkness deepens, it makes no difference if that darkness is a bombing raid that lasts all night, an illness that stretches over ten years, or death itself—when God promised to abide, He is saying He'll be there through all our need and then beyond.

The verb "abide," when connected with the preposition "in," speaks in the third place of the amazing *intimacy* of the relationship we and God can have. Not even a father and son, a husband and wife, are this close. They "abide *with*" one another, but not *in*. With Christ the companionship is closer still. In the fifteenth chapter of St. John's Gospel, when Jesus speaks of himself as the vine and us as the branches, over and over again He uses these words "abide in," showing that they tell of a relationship that becomes a union. In the Baptismal service in our church this morning you will hear this sacrament described as an "engrafting into Christ," as when a branch is transplanted and made a part of another tree. In Communion we take the wine and the bread into our bodies, to show how the presence of Christ in incorporated into our souls. These are all various means of pointing toward the intimate connection it is possible for you and me to have with our God summed up in "abide."

But how can you know if you have such fellowship? Most of us go through high moments when God seems near, and again times of despair when we doubt if He even exists. Such moods are not dependable indexes of our actual status with God. But St. John gives us three valid measurements to use which will help us know just where we stand.

First, "By this we know that we abide in him and he in us, because he has given us of his own Spirit." Now the Spirit can never be seen. Neither can the rays of the sun. Yet men who have worked in the summer sun bear the mark of the sun by skin with a deep tan. People who are surrounded and infused by the Spirit of God also bear certain marks. He is the Spirit of Truth, and if you have received Him you will always be searching for truth by asking deep and profound questions, often disturbing ones, about the nature of this world, what God is like, the meaning of life. He is the Spirit of prayer, and if you are living in His presence you will be a man of prayer, one who manages to find time somehow each day to pray, one who regards these moments as the high point of life. The Holy Spirit leads men to have confidence and trust, and if you have received this offered gift God will not seem to you remote and aloof so that you are afraid much of the time, but you will be confidently saying to Him, "Abba, Father." And the Spirit of God also brings warmth and radiance to cold hearts. If he has taken over your heart Christianity will not be just a set of laws or a philosophy of life about which you can look weary and grim and dour; but there will be a sparkle in your eyes and a smile on your face. Do you have these marks of the Spirit about you? You know whether your face is bronzed by the end of the summer. I think you can know also whether you bear the marks of one who lives in the climate of the Spirit of God. And if you do, this is a first indication that you are abiding in Him and He in you.

But this is a rather subjective test, one in which many of us delude ourselves into thinking we're more than we are. The second standard St. John holds up is "Whoever confesses that Jesus is the Son of God, God abides in him, and he in God." Here we come out of the realm of thought and feeling into that of speech and witness, for that is what "confesses" means. People who are as close to God as "abide in" suggests, just will be found talking about Him to friends and relatives, yes and to strangers too. A dictator does not lack courage to speak when he is backed up by tanks and guns. A Christian does not lack courage to be an evangelist when he knows he is backed by the power of almighty God. Nor does he lack for something to say. He confesses that Jesus is the Son of God and that is enough. He may not be smooth and polished in his delivery, or eloquent in his choice of words. But if God is abiding in him, and he in God, he has a message to deliver—that God is like Jesus. The habit of making such a witness or testimony is a sign that the relationship with God is sound and strong. If you are making opportunities for "speaking a good word for the Lord," rejoice, for your connection with Him almost certainly is close. If not, it is time to ask what is wrong between you and Him.

The third test is not subjective, nor is it verbal, but it is ethical. "God is love, and he who abides in love abides in God and God abides in him." Love here of course does not mean affection or romance. We refer to love such as was found in Christ Jesus—an unselfish concern for the welfare of another whether he is appealing or not, for all others whether they welcome our attention or not. This is how God loved us; this is the way we are to love other people. No human being has the ability in himself to love with this kind of love. Like electrical power, love is dependent each instant upon a continuing source of supply. This love is in us when God abides in us; it is not there if we have shut him out. Tenderness may be there; parental affection; romance. But not Christ's kind of love. So when such love is in any life, we know that God is dwelling there. Is such a love a part of you? Does it flow from you like water from a mountain spring? If it does, then you can know that you are abiding in God, and He in you.

I'm afraid that a great many of you hardly know what I am talking about when I speak of God's abiding presence—this is beyond your realm of experience—you have flunked the test and admit there is a void in your soul. But fortunately the three tests I've mentioned are not just signs of what exists, but also conditions of getting what you lack. Begin now to try to love the unlovely, to speak to others what you do know about God, to reflect the presence of the Holy Spirit in habits of prayer—and you will soon find a companion in your life who will abide forever.

Does It Really Matter?

Date: April 17, 1960—Easter

Lectionary: Psalm 118; **I Corinthians 15:1-19**;
St. Matthew 28:1-15

Hymns: "Jesus Christ Is Risen Today," "Thine Is The Glory" and
"The Day of Resurrection"

If Christ has not been raised, then our preaching is in vain and your faith is in vain." In that prize winning movie of a couple of years back, "The Bridge on the River Kwai," the commando unit of Allied soldiers who were sent to destroy the key railroad trestle the Japanese had managed to construct in the jungles of Burma with the help of prisoner of war labor had to know not only how to set off explosives, but against just which pilings they should be placed. For in the construction of a bridge some support can be removed with only minor damage ensuing, while other piers and beams are so vital that if they are removed the whole structure will collapse. Nor is this true of bridges alone. Take away the keystone of an arch that has stood for centuries and it will soon crumble to the ground. Remove the mother from a home and normally family life will cease to exist. Take away the resurrection, and as St. Paul warned the Corinthians, the Christian faith becomes an empty shell.

Perhaps you never realized before it was quite so important. Some people would say "Still we have the great moral teachings of

Jesus even if the resurrection is not true." But He who taught men to love their enemies, to sell all their goods, to be meek and humble, also said to His disciples that when he went up to Jerusalem He would be crucified and on the third day be raised again. (Matthew 16:21). If the resurrection is not true, and He cannot be trusted in regard to it, how can we be sure we want to risk our lives and welfare in obeying His call to love or poverty or humility? Others of you might say, "But the moral teachings of Jesus are not the core of the Gospel, it's His death on the cross that really counts, and that was complete before the resurrection took place." Yet look at the Cross and see what it would mean without the empty tomb. From the human point of view Christ's willingness to die for His cause would, without the resurrection, appear like Don Quixote's fight against the windmill—an extravagant but fruitless gesture in which "It is finished" signifies defeat rather than the completion of a mission. If you think of the crucifixion in terms of God, the Cross on Friday without the appearance of a Risen Lord on the first day of the week would make God appear as cruel and heartless as a little boy who pulls off the wings of insects to watch them wiggle and die. Calvary too loses its meaning without Easter to turn it into triumph.

And certainly the widespread hope found among men that there is something beyond the grave, the almost universal protest of those who are faced with the death of a loved one that "This must not be the end"—all this too becomes just an empty shell "if Christ has not been raised" for nothing is more precarious than hope built on nothing more than wishful thinking or groundless dreams. When I was a boy there used to be a popular song which ran, "Wishing will make it so, just keep on wishing and cares will go." Many people today base their lives on nothing more solid than this. In wishing to be rich they live as though they had money, and they spend happily in a world of illusion, until suddenly their world of pretense falls in on them. The freedom fighters of Hungary, in 1957, gambled their lives and homes in the belief that if they began a rebellion against Russia America must come to their aid. Their

54

hope was strong, and inspiring indeed, but it had no foundation. They went down into ruin. And simply the fact that people want there to be a life beyond death, just because they count on it for years and depend upon it in their last hours, is no guaranty whatsoever that it's really waiting for them beyond. As St. Paul went on to say, "If…we…have only hope, we are of all men most to be pitied." And without the resurrection there is nothing more substantial we can have than hope. Only when Vasco da Gama returned with treasure from India in about the year 1500 did the age old dream of an all-water route from Europe to the East prove to be something more substantial than hope. Only when the beep-beep of Sputnik I could be heard on short-wave radios did space travel become for the American public a matter worth serious consideration. And perhaps it is right that we should be skeptical. Thousands of people in the Middle Ages were impoverished by alchemists who duped them into hoping that lead could be transformed into gold. Whereas da Gama's hope of sailing to India was based upon a possibility, the Spanish explorer De Soto lost his life, and was buried in the Mississippi River not too far from here, in a vain search for cities of gold which he could not find because they never existed. I would not encourage you to have any hope for life behind the grave unless some evidence can be found that such a life really exists. And the only reliable evidence we have is in Christ who was raised from the tomb. Of course there is Lazarus; and the widow's son whom Jesus revived. But about them we know almost nothing, while of Jesus as He was after physical death we know a good deal. Those who believe in Him have a foundation for hope that is far more than wishful thinking and dreaming. It is based upon fact and knowledge and experience. Were it not for His resurrection we who know we must someday die, we who have lost those we love, would be of all men most to be pitied, for our hope would be just wishing.

But, perhaps you are saying, "Do we really know that He was raised from the dead?" There is no photograph of the empty tomb, and even had one been taken it could be possible that the body was stolen, as the Roman soldiers said. And how dependable is the testimony of those to whom Jesus appeared? Mary Magdalene had once been a prostitute—is it unreasonable to wonder if she might not now take up lying? Peter had been an intimate friend, and on top of that had a terrible sense of guilt for having denied Jesus three times. Could it be that in his grief he just imagined things? Yes, all these things are possible. In terms of scientific evidence and legal proof, no one is going to be forced into accepting the reality of the resurrection of Christ. But one thing you'll have a hard time getting around is the historical fact of the Church, and the sudden transformation of the disciples and women who first reported it. They were not simply telling each other things they had previously believed. It is true Jesus had foretold he would be raised on the third day, but apparently not a one of them really heard or understood. St. Luke tells us Mary and the other women went to the Garden early in the morning with no other thought than to embalm the body of One they loved. When they rushed into Jerusalem to tell the apostles that Jesus was alive, St. Luke indicates those sorrowing disciples didn't even bother to check into what they considered was an idle tale. When two men were joined that evening by Jesus as they walked to the village of Emmaus they did not even recognize Him until they sat together and broke bread. No— there is no reason to believe that the disciples were hallucinating because of preconceived ideas that this must take place. They were startled and surprised when Jesus appeared.

That something took place in their lives is beyond all dispute. Men who were weak suddenly became strong. Peter, who had denied, at last grew into the rock which was his nickname. A discouraged and defeated handful, locked in a room in Jerusalem for fear of the Jews, suddenly emerged as a courageous army who dared to preach in the Temple about Jesus, and defied priests and kings who ordered them to cease. How else can you explain it if something new had not entered their lives? When Marie and Pierre Curie, the Polish scientists living in Paris, discovered that photographic plates exposed to a certain type of pitch reacted in a way which could not be explained, they asked themselves if there could not be a force hidden in that pitch of which science had no knowledge. They were ridiculed and scorned, but something kept happing to the photographic plates. This transformation must somehow be explained. And finally the existence of radium was discovered and proved. This I would say is the only way you are really going to come to believe that Christ is alive in this world. Take a life which is transformed and study it carefully. Check all possible explanations until none is left except the one claimed by the man who has been changed—namely that he no longer walks alone, but in the presence of the Risen Christ. Or better yet—take your own life, if you have been changed. To St. Paul the most dramatic proof was his own reformation following an experience on the way to Damascus. To me the unshakable proof is the liberation I have known from certain prejudices and hates. From your life, if you have heard the Risen Christ say "Hail," there will come similar testimony that can help others believe. We, whom He has addressed, can account for our new lives in no other way. We know that Christ is risen. He is risen indeed—and this has on our faith marvelous effects. The moral teachings we admire now have authority. The Cross on which we meditated now appears as a victory for Jesus, and speaks of love instead of cruelty at the heart of God. The hope of life beyond death is no longer just the aching desire of a grief stricken heart—it is based on the knowledge of One who Himself died and was returned from the dead.

But eternal life which is no more than existence that never ends could be a horror and curse rather than a blessing and source of hope. We all know people for whom death was, or would be, a release. We would be dismayed and distressed if we thought life beyond for them would continue as it has been. It is not enough to know there *is* a life, but the heart yearns to know what *kind* of life it will be. Some of us in this congregation have asked this question most urgently in the last year. The answers we receive will always be partial—will never fully satisfy. Later in the 15th chapter of I Corinthians St. Paul writes of terrestrial bodies and celestial bodies; of physical bodies and spiritual bodies. The nature of the one is as different from the other as the poppy seed planted in the ground is from the beautiful red flower that blossoms above the earth. We who are still in the lower order cannot see through into the next. But Christ, in his Post-resurrection appearances, gave us some hints.

First, in the life hereafter people will be recognizable and will have concern for their loved ones. The women in the Garden knew who Jesus was the moment He said "Hail"; even St. Paul who had never seen Jesus in the flesh, on the road to Damascus identified him at once. And Jesus in His conversations showed concern for His friends' welfare. He told the women not to be afraid. He sent messages to the disciples as a group, and to individuals like Peter and Thomas. When we anticipate eternal life in Christ for ourselves or those know, we can find great comfort because personal ties will still be strong.

Second, in the life beyond, which we enter through Christ, there is forgiveness of sins—no carry-over of wrongs. The eleven who had forsaken Him, each in his own way, Jesus called brethren—a term of reconciliation. The thief on the neighboring cross who apparently had been a criminal rouge for years was promised life that day which was described by the word Paradise. Peter, who had denied Him, Jesus restored by entrusting to him the care of the sheep. We are relieved to know that in life beyond death grudges are not held, or wrongs remembered.

Third, those who fear they might be bored doing nothing, or even sitting in the presence of God if it lasts forever, should find in Christ's resurrection appearances evidence that the life after this is one of great activity. Read over them for yourself. Christ is forever giving orders and directions—go, tell, meet me, feed my sheep, touch my wounds, cast your nets on the other side of the boat. This would indicate to me that life beyond is one of service and obedience.

Fourth, the dominant notes in Christ's conversation after He was raised from the dead are those of joy and peace, but primarily joy. There is no fear; there is no loneliness; there is no fatigue in those who do His work for He supplies the power that is needed. The word with which the Lord addressed the women in the Garden that morning is translated in our Bibles as "Hail," but literally it means "be glad, rejoice." Remember this always when death comes near your home. There may be tears on this side, but the first word spoken on the other is "Hail," rejoice.

"If Christ has not been raised, then our preaching is in vain and your faith is in vain." But Christ has risen. He is risen indeed. The faith is sound in all its parts, but I would especially say to you this day that hope for a life beyond death need never be questioned by you who know and live in the risen Christ.

GRACE PRESBYTERIAN CHURCH

Little Rock, Arkansas

ALTERNATING CURRENT

Date: July 16, 1961—Seventh Sunday after Trinity

Lectionary: Psalm 84; Lamentations 3:19-41; **St. Mark 6:30-56**

Hymns: "Holy, Holy, Holy," "The Lord's My Shepherd"
       (Crimond), "Prayer Is The Soul's Sincere Desire"

"And he said to them, 'Come away by yourselves to a lonely place, and rest a while.' For many were coming and going, and they had no leisure even to eat. And they went away in the boat to a lonely place by themselves." Then after the feeding of the five thousand, "Immediately he made his disciples get into the boat and go before him to the other side…while he dismissed the crowd. And after he had taken leave of them, he went into the hills to pray."

The sixth chapter of St. Mark's Gospel is fairly typical of those passages which attempt to convey to us some understanding of the life of Jesus Christ. In it we find a rhythm or pattern in which we are taken from activity to prayer to activity back to prayer again. In the electrical world there are, I believe, two types of current—DC and AC. Direct Current is fine for short distances but if you want electricity to go very far you always use Alternating Current. You engineers may have to set me straight when church is over, but it is my understanding that the tremendous energy which comes to us across miles of copper wiring is the result of very rapid alternation between negative and positive charges in the generator. Transposing this over into the spiritual realm of life, the power of Jesus Christ, and the power in every Christian life if it is going to last for any length of time, is always of the Alternating Current type.

When our Scripture lesson begins the disciples have just re-turned from what was probably their first teaching and healing mis-sion. Jesus says, "Come away by yourselves to a lonely place, and rest a while." Then when they get to the lonely place they find that it isn't lonely anymore for the people walked around the end of the lake faster than the little band could row across it. Jesus has com-passion on them—preaching to them and then finally feeding the whole multitude with the miracle of the five loaves and two fish. But soon the basic rhythm of life is displayed when He dismisses all and strikes out to the hills to pray. After about nine hours by Himself with the Father once more Jesus is called upon to serve by saving the disciples in the boat from the dangers of a storm that had swept down on the Sea of Galilee. And immediately upon their landing the next morning He was deluged with requests to heal the sick from towns and villages from miles around. All this He was able to do because He had spent the night before in prayer. Just look at the things for which he was equipped by a life of prayer to do—training the twelve as evangelists and granting them au-thority, preaching with such power that five thousand people were held spellbound for most of a day, feeding this multitude in some miraculous way we do not understand, controlling the elements of the storm and walking upon the waters, healing the sick even by the touch of his garments.

One of the great heresies, or wrong beliefs, of modern Christianity is the assumption that the wonderful deeds of Jesus are due to His divine nature, and that we—because we are just human—can only admire them from afar. D. S. Cairns, a Scottish theologian, in a book entitled *A Faith That Rebels* points out quite clearly that this is not so. Jesus did these things not by virtue of being the Son of God, but because He was filled with the Holy Spirit. And the same Holy Spirit has been offered to you and me, just as it was to the early disciples, if we will but let Him in our lives. Just check through the Bible and you'll find that everything Jesus did in this sixth chapter of St. Mark, except calming the storm, was done by someone else, not divine, whose heart was opened to the Holy Spirit. Peter and John and Philip healed the sick; Peter walked on the water; he preached to multitudes on Pentecost and converted three thousand that day. Even the feeding of the five thousand has a parallel in the life of Elisha as told in the fourth chapter of II Kings. The limits on our power to do great things for God have not been imposed on us by Him; they are the result of our refusal to enter into the alternating rhythm of service and prayer which was demonstrated for us in the life of Jesus. Some few people in the Church pray all the time and don't do anything. Though they are less effective than they might be, let's don't waste our time chastising them for I haven't seen too many of them out in this Rodney Parham area! The bulk of us modern day Christians want instead always to be *doing* something and can't be bothered with any serious experiments in prayer. We say we don't have the time for much more than a "Now I lay me down to sleep" and a hurried mumbling of the Lord's Prayer. How wrong we are! If you'll read the biography of any one of the great Christian leaders of our own day you'll find that every one of them does find or *make* time to talk with God without rushing. The more they get done nearly always the more time they have spent on their knees. Kagawa, the Japanese saint, had to get by on three or four hours of sleep a night to do it—but he knew without prayer his preaching, his writing, his slum clearance work would collapse. Jesus made this very clear two thousand years ago. Tremendous power and authority await those who develop a rhythm of life of prayer and work. We who decline to enter into it do grieve God, but what might be more per- suasive to those of us whose hearts are hardened—we render our- selves impotent. In a matter of months or at most a few years, we'll no longer be able to do those good works, to fulfill those urgent assignments which right now are pointing us in only one direction. But it is not too late even now to change. If you will serve, and also pray, you will find the strength that has begun to ebb flowing back into you as the doors are once more opened to the entrance of the Holy Spirit—and somehow there'll be more time than ever to do the things God wants you to do.

Now if you are going to try to develop the prayer side of life there are at least two aspects of it you ought to include. The first, and the one you all have some acquaintance with, is the individual type of prayer. Jesus said, "When you pray, go into your room and shut the door" (Matthew 6:6). In the chapter before us this morning you will remember that Jesus sent His disciples off in a boat, and then dismissed the multitude of five thousand—and set off into the hills *all by Himself to pray.* You know, there are some people in this world who are by themselves so seldom that they are scared at the thought of being alone with God. Part of this is because in our small, modern houses there's no opportunity for privacy indoors, and those of us in the city have no escape in the woods or fields. But somehow you *must* find some solitude if you are going to grow in the life of prayer. Don't be led astray by thinking that you can start right off like Brother Lawrence, the medieval monk, who said he could practice the presence of God as well while working in the kitchen as he could before the Blessed Sacrament. There's a poem about William Blake, the mystical poet:

> *He came to the desert of London town,*
> *Grey miles long.*
> *He wandered up and he wandered down,*
> *Singing a quiet song.*
> *He came to the desert of London town,*
> *Murk miles broad.*
> *He wandered up and he wandered down,*
> *Ever alone with God. (IB, VII, 739)*

This kind of solitude in the midst of a hubbub is a special gift to those who are "far ben" in the life of prayer—to Brother Lawrence, and William Blake—and a businessman I knew in New Haven who prayed daily behind the *New York Times* while commuting to work on the train. You may reach this stage eventually, but to start with, all people, and for most of us throughout life, there must be silence and solitude. I hope, when we build our new church, there will be at least one room open at all times to anyone who needs a place to pray. Until then it may mean that you simply will have to ask your family to honor the closed door of your bedroom during a certain hour of the day—and in return, promise to grant them the same right at another point in the daily schedule. Don't be shy about it; don't feel that it is selfish for you to ask this. Jesus sent five thousand people home, just so He could pray. Or it may mean that you'll have to set the alarm and get up before the children wake; or stay up at night after everyone else has gone to bed. Jesus often was forced to do these things—in this chapter we are told He prayed until three in morning, and on another occasion He rose before it was day. I want to talk more in another sermon about *what* you do once you're alone in a room with God. But right now let me just urge you to get there—and be still. Take with you a Bible, a book of prayers or devotional guide to prime the pump—and just wait for twenty or thirty minutes. For a few days you'll think you're going crazy—but before long I'm convinced something will begin to happen.

Individual prayer is essential—but it is never enough for one who is seriously interested in the Christian life. Olive Wyon has written, "Although prayer is an intensely *personal* matter, it is not *individualistic*." There were occasions when Jesus wanted to be alone; there were other times when He sought refreshment with a small group of intimate friends. "And they went away in the boat to a lonely place by themselves." He knew the role of solitude; He esteemed the place of the larger fellowship of the Church—for He never missed an opportunity to go to synagogue or temple. But in the prayer life of Jesus there was a need for something in between, when He could meet with the Father in the presence of just a few kindred spirits. We find that here when they crossed the Sea of Galilee. Again He wanted it on the Mount of Transfiguration when He took along just Peter and James and John. And part of the time in Gethsemane he asked for the company of the inner three. Even our Lord found that the spiritual fellowship was stronger with some than with others. Down through the centuries Christians have had similar experiences. Small groups have come together not as rivals to the Church, but as supplements. They have been called "the church within the church." In early Methodism they were called "class meetings." Forty years ago many were called "Oxford Groups." In our own generation they are usually termed prayer groups or cell groups. (In recent years the anti-communist movement has become so rabid that many people are scared of the word "cell"—they'll probably quit using it in biology pretty soon! But don't be afraid of Christian cell groups. There's nothing subversive about them at all, I can assure you.) A number of people feel that these small groups are the most promising hope for Christianity in the mid-twentieth century. Down through Church history we know for a fact that the mass movements of one generation nearly always have issued from small groups who in the previous generation met for prayer and study and action. Such groups are meeting all over the world. In Communist China and East Germany the organized Church can be watched and controlled, but no secret police can stop two to twelve people from meeting in a basement. These little Christian gatherings can be found in homes where housewives gather, at hotels where businessmen meet for lunch and prayer, in dormitories and barracks. There is nothing like the inspiration that comes from this kind of fellowship. I was in four or five different prayer groups during my college and seminary days. I received a strength which I have lacked ever since. I hope and pray that some in this congregation will feel moved by God to "come away to a lonely place" where we can meet for prayer.

There are just a few rules that have to be laid down. The group must be small—twelve I think is the maximum. It can't be organized. Those who come must come regularly, giving this appointment with God priority equal to or above that of an appointment with the President of the United States. Those who join a prayer group should not try to mix this with coffee and socializing. Those who are prepared for this intimate fellowship in prayer should be prepared to explore, knowing that God will lead them into depths of communion that are heretofore unknown and that sometimes are frightening. I have some books and pamphlets on prayer groups which those of you who are interested are welcomed to read. Frankly, I hunger for this kind of thing. I think our church will never be deep until there are many such groups meeting. Excuses about waiting until a more convenient time don't hold water, for there will never be a convenient time. Those of you who sense the need will make time. And when you do, things will begin to happen in Grace Church that we have not known before.

The strength of Christ came from an alternating pattern of activity—of service and prayer and service. The strength of every Christian is dependant upon the same rhythm. *All* of us must go to God in solitary prayer and in the corporate worship of the church; *many* of us will also want to go apart with a few other kindred spirits. I call on you to re-examine your own prayer life this day.

Under Threat of Nuclear War

Date: October 28, 1962—19th Sunday after Trinity,
"Reformation Sunday"

Lectionary: **Psalm 91**; II Kings 19:22-34; St. Matthew 10:34-42

Hymns: "A Mighty Fortress," "I Look To Thee In Every Need,"
"Faith of Our Fathers"

On October 16, 1962 President John F. Kennedy was notified of an aerial photograph taken two days before showing Russian missiles installed in Cuba. In a television talk on October 22 he notified the American public a naval blockade of Cuba had been set up to prevent Russian support. During the "Cuban Missile Crisis" the world teetered on the brink of nuclear war. This sermon was written on October 27 and preached the following morning, October 28. Later that day a settlement was announced.

"He who dwells in the shelter of the Most High, who abides in the shadow of the Almighty, will say to the Lord, 'My refuge and my fortress; my God, in whom I trust.'"

On Reformation Day, those of us who know even the slightest bit of church history find our minds turning back to the events that took place during that century and a half after 1517 when Martin Luther nailed his Ninety-Five Theses on the door of the castle church in Wittenberg, Germany. These decades were dominated by Luther and Calvin, Bunyan and Cromwell who differed with each other on a great many points, but in one way they were all alike—and later generations have never been able to forget. They had courage under adversity and when all their dreams and hopes, their very world, seemed to be collapsing, they maintained an inner peace and calm.

Although Luther, in October of 1517, did not intend to start such a revolution as his spark ignited, at first it seemed that success was to be his nevertheless. Then the tide began to turn. The Pope issued a bull excommunicating Luther. A Diet, or congress of German princes, was called at the city of Worms. Luther was tried and condemned and placed under ban of the empire. He was a hunted man apparently doomed to end in futile martyrdom. On his way back from Worms, when all looked so hopeless, he was suddenly kidnapped by men whose identity he did not know. Soon he discovered that he was captured for his own good—for he was taken to the castle of Wartburg and hidden from Pope and Emperor. He assumed a false name and disguised himself with a beard. But even with these precautions, discovery, capture and torture were never far away. On top of his personal danger, reports reached him that things were not going well with the new movement. The reforming leaders in Wittenberg were getting at odds with one another. To many a man the situation would have seemed desperate. But out of this grew the great Reformation hymn, "A mighty fortress is our God, a bulwark never failing; our helper He amid the flood of mortal ills prevailing." Martin Luther never wavered. He never gave up in the face of odds that to us would seem overwhelming.

Some hundred years later Germany was still being torn by religious strife in the Thirty Years War. Protestant forces in the north fought with Catholics ones in the south. From 1618 to 1648 this poor land was devastated by the besieging of cities, the march of armies across fields ready to harvest, and the destruction of centers of learning. On top of that Europe during these years was hit by the Black Death, an epidemic of bubonic plague that recurred year after year. Of course no one knew about germs; no one had any idea of the cause. The population of Germany dropped from sixteen million to six as a result of war and the Black Death combined. People locked themselves in their houses and refused to let their neighbors enter, even though they might be starving to death. Living in Germany at this point in history was for most folks as much like hell as anything could possibly be. Yet in the midst of it all, a few people never feared or grew disheartened. One of them, a pastor named Martin Rinkart who had buried most of his congregation, sat down in the midst of war, epidemic and hysteria to write a poem we still sing as a hymn, "Now thank we all our God with heart and hands and voices, who wondrous things hath done, in whom the world rejoices." How could this be, perhaps you are asking? Where can men like Luther and Rinkart find such tranquility?

One of the sources to which they looked most often was Psalm 91—"He who dwells in the shelter of the Most High, who abides in the shadow of the Almighty, will say to the Lord, 'My refuge and my fortress, my God, in whom I trust.'" These German pastors may have wondered why this Psalm spoke to their condition so perfectly. We know through Biblical scholarship it was because it was composed in a situation so similar to their own. The scholars think it was written by and for the Jewish exiles inside Babylon at the time when Persia was about to take that city. It turned out later that the Persians were more lenient rulers than the Babylonians, but at this point no one knew this. Uncertainty often makes men imagine the worst, and many of the Jews probably did. And even if the victors were generous, war is always a horrible experience, especially on the inside of a besieged city where death may come by lingering starvation. Can you not picture in your mind's eye the consternation that must have run through the Jewish community as the Persian army approached? Can you see little knots of anxious people gathered to exchange rumors sweeping the city? Then to the disturbed community comes a song out of the heart of one man who lived very close to God. "He who dwells in the shelter of the Most High, who abides in the shadow of the Almighty, will say to the Lord, 'My refuge and my fortress, my God, in whom I trust.'" And slowly the panic subsides. The lit-

72

tle groups of people scatter and go home. The battle on the outside of the city walls begins. But within the hearts of God's people a peace slowly spreads, a peace that cannot be shaken.

Once more we need to turn to this great psalm. Within the past week international relations have taken a sudden turn for the worse, and we now stand right at the brink of war. If war comes it will apparently be not with so called conventional weapons, but nuclear arms since they are the matter in dispute. So we face the danger of a blast that will level everything for miles; the danger of fallout; the possibility that germ warfare will be employed. You and I who are adults know these things—and so do all you children old enough to listen to TV. Housewives are rushing to the stores to stock up on supplies; a little girl on the playground at Brady School the other day came in tears to her teacher, she was so upset and fearful over the talk she had been hearing. Even on the kinder-garten level the children are discussing it. What does the Christian Gospel have to say when the situation does indeed look dark; when fear is abroad in our land? Four things I would say to you today.

First of all, I want to talk to you about death. The Psalmist promises us that "a thousand may fall at your side, ten thousand at your right hand; but it will not come near you." And certainly it is true that the faithful many times seem to be guided or strength-ened so that they survive in impossible situations. Martin Luther in hiding and Martin Rinkart burying victims of the Black Death are two cases in point. But it is not always so. Stephen, the first Christian martyr, was stoned to death by a mob in Jerusalem. Dietrich Bonhoeffer was killed by the Nazis in 1945 only a few days before he would have been liberated. Belief in God is no good luck charm guaranteed to work in all situations. After all, you must re-member that every one will some day die. I grant you that it is hard for us to conceive of this world going on without us, but we know that it will. So the question is not *whether* I die, but when and how and why. And even the matter of "when" loses its significance in comparison with "how" and "why." It really makes little difference to me, personally, whether I die today or fifty years from now, if the end comes while I am in the spirit and service of Jesus Christ; if the end is brought about because I am doing His will. Of course I would like to live in order to serve my family and the Church. But as far as I am concerned death has no fear. I believe that if in this life I am with God, beyond death I shall be also. The change is nothing to fear. God is our refuge and fortress against death, not by abolishing it—but by removing from His loved ones any terror of the unknown. No man can be afraid to walk through the valley of the shadow if he knows that he does not walk alone. I hope each of you present this morning has the assurance of God's presence in such measure that the question of your own death should war strike is of no real consequence to you.

Second, I want to say to you that survival of material goods, or even of family, is not the most important thing on earth. Martin Luther in his great hymn wrote, "Let goods and kindred go, this mortal life also; the body they may kill: God's truth abideth still; His kingdom is forever." I think most of us are prepared to give at least lip service to the statement that the material things of this world don't count in the final analysis. We say that human values come way ahead of houses and bank accounts and heirlooms and factories in which we own stock. We *say* this—although we spend most of our time and energy acquiring and caring for these material things to the neglect of the persons for whom we acquire them. But assuming that what we say is what we truly feel—are we prepared to go one step further and give up not only our goods but our kindred too? At the mere suggestion, most of us grow angry. For we in America have developed a family cult that says the home must come first, before anything else. Yet Jesus did not so teach. He said "He who loves father or mother more than me is not worthy of me; and he who loves son or daughter more than me is not worthy of me." So while a Christian of course wants his family to survive, it is far better that not only we but our family also perish rather than resort to means and ends contrary to the will of God. This may seem shocking to you at first. But if you believe in life beyond death not only for yourself but for others; and if you believe that this life is given to those in harmony with Christ's spirit—it becomes far more important to live in honesty and charity, in meekness and generosity, even if it be for just a short time—than it is to eek out an existence over many years by means of lying and hoarding, or brutality and hate. The Christian is prepared to sacrifice not only his worldly goods but even his family's physical survival rather than to lead them contrary to Christ's way. For he knows that when this way is followed his family will receive, perhaps in this world but certainly in the next, a life far richer than he could have won for them by other means. So if the thought of providing for your family has become a matter of primary concern for you at this point in world history—if you cannot sleep at night for fear you have not taken sufficient precautions to insure their survival—hear this. There is a life far more important for which you can provide. See that you take care of this first. If there is time for stockpiling, building bomb shelters, then well and good. But physical survival for your family, if they do not think honestly, speak charitably and behave generously is a living hell. Better they die in loving obedience to God than survive in selfishness.

A third thing I would say to you. Don't hit the panic button and devote all your efforts to survival in the face of a disaster, when disaster has not yet come. It is true that the day seems to be far spent, and the night of fear and hostility appears to be drawing close. But darkness has not fallen, and unlike the movement of the planet, the direction of world affairs can be reversed. To change the figure of speech, in the medical world the prognosis may be very poor, but the doctors and nurses never stop working so long as a patient is still alive. If you are deeply concerned about the dangers of world war, devote your efforts to preservation of peace rather than to your personal survival during war. If all the hours with neighbors discussing what to do in case of attack had instead been devoted to prayers for the leaders of the nations; if the money spent on extra food and hideaways were invested in the world mission enterprise; if the self-righteous examination of the sins of Russia and Cuba were turned toward the injustices still existing in our own nation so that the uncommitted people of the world would not so easily take offense—if our time and money and energies were redirected toward the winning of peace rather than preparing for disaster, war might never come. But you say, "It's such a gamble." Of course it is a gamble—it's a long, long shot. But it was Jesus who said, "He who finds his life will lose it, and he who loses his life for my sake will find it." The way of Christ is always risky. But what other path would you rather follow?

And now my fourth word to you. The God in whom we trust is "Most High" and He is "Almighty." All that I have said before hinges upon this fact. If this is not true, then my casual attitude toward my own death is foolishness, and I am offering to step into oblivion. If this is not true, in sacrificing my worldly goods and even my family to a way of life which Jesus taught, I am living in a world of illusion and am deceiving the people I love most. If this is not true, my attempts to turn back a tidal wave of hatred with a few deeds of love is stupidity, and I should be spending these last minutes digging a hole in which to hide. But if it *is* true that God is King and rules with power, then my apparent foolishness is not stupid at all. Perhaps it even partakes of the foolishness of God that is wiser than men. It might share something of the Spirit of Him who came in weakness and humility to overcome an arrogant world. It seemed on Good Friday that His efforts had all been in vain. On Saturday the disciples were without hope. And then the tide began to turn. From death there came life; from hatred love arose unblemished; from weakness there issued a power which no kingdom or war has ever stopped. I believe this same God rules today, and I believe He rules with the same methods. This does not say that war may not come. It does not say that powers of atheism and brutality may not have their day. But the Good News of Jesus Christ does say that ultimately God will win, and He'll win by the means Jesus Christ marked out. They are the way of meekness, of self-sacrifice, yes even of sacrifice of those we love. But they are eternal ways that spring up out of unlimited power from on high. God will win. If we desert him out of fear we may delay the time a bit. But God will rule. I know this. And I for one want to be one of His loyal servants. I had far rather do this than simply survive. I do not say by this to ignore all simple precautions. But I do say, be calm. Be trustful. God is still King. Those of you who do not know Him well, who do not live in him, will think I'm talking gibberish today. But those of you who are prepared to take the leap of faith, to live in Christ, will know I speak the truth. And to you there will come peace in the midst of a storm, and peace though all seems to pass away.

Ten Years After Ordination

Date: June 23, 1963—Second Sunday after Trinity,

Lectionary: Psalm 103; Isaiah 61:1-11; **Ephesians 3:1-13**

Hymns: "Praise The Lord, His Glories Show," "Come, Christians, Join To Sing," "God of the Prophets"

Tenth anniversary of my ordination to the ministry.

"Of this gospel I was made a minister according to the gift of God's grace which was given me by the working of his power. To me, though I am the very least of all the saints, this grace was given, to preach to the Gentiles the unsearchable riches of Christ."

As I said last Sunday in the announcements, on June 21, 1953 I was ordained to the Gospel ministry by a commission of Washburn Presbytery in the sanctuary of the Second Presbyterian Church of this city. With your indulgence, I'd like this morning to reflect on the ministry as it looks ten years later. It has done me good to take stock, and I hope it will be of some benefit to you to look through the eyes of another into this office with which you have such frequent dealings.

The first thing I want to say is that after this passage of time, I am more sure than ever that what the Good News tells us is true. I believed it ten years ago when I was ordained—but many facets of the Gospel were pure theory then. Events of the past ten years have confirmed me in the central aspects of the faith. Oh, as you know, I still have a lot of unanswered questions. Frankly, I hope thirty years from now I will still have areas in which I'm probing, for a man who has no doubts left, no frontiers to explore, is intellectually and spiritually dead. But these matters usually lie on the periphery. At the center of the Gospel there's a body of truth about which I am more and more certain. Don't react in righteous surprise that I feel it necessary even to say this. For there are ministers of my age who are going through plain hell because they are not sure. They mouth the words they are expected to say but it has become quite unreal to them. I note this, not in condemnation but in pity. Some of them have had experiences that have disillusioned them, that have shaken their very foundations—experiences I've not sampled. I do not know how I would react under their circumstances. I hope I would have the honesty and courage to quit the ministry if I could not put my whole heart in what I was proclaiming. I'm just thankful that I've never had to decide—that these ten years, instead of whittling away at my faith have built it up bit by bit.

Let me give two or three illustrations of what I mean. I started out with a belief that all men are sinners in need of salvation—in the words of St. Paul, "all have sinned and fall short of the glory of God." (Romans 3:23). After several hundred counseling interviews, and at least two hundred session meetings (as well as many hours of looking into my own soul), I *know* this is so. There are a lot of folks who according to the world's standards are righteous; who put on a mighty good show of virtue for the public. But I've never seen one yet who wasn't touched with pride or greed or bitterness. And most, once they trust you, will admit that this is so. I'm more certain than ever that all men are sinners in need of forgiveness.

But this is matched by a growing confidence in the reality of that forgiveness. It's fine to read passages of Scripture that say "though your sins are like scarlet they shall be a white as snow," and to hear Jesus in the story of the woman taken in adultery remark "neither do I condemn you. Go and sin no more." But I used to wonder if it could really happen—if there were not some sins too heinous to cover over. My years in the ministry so far have not revealed a single deed or thought or word too big for God to handle. Oh, I've seen a lot of them remain in lives, festering and causing all kinds of trouble because there was never any honest confession or sincere repentance and amendment of life. But where there has been true remorse and trust, miracles have taken place. A man committed adultery with his wife's best friend. For a time it seemed as though there could be no reconciliation—but when it was all over, the marriage was stronger than ever, and the man was walking close to God. I could cite dozens of other examples. When I preach to you that God can forgive anything I'm not only echoing words of Scripture. I'm also testifying what I have seen with my eyes and experienced in my heart.

And I'm also more sure than ever of the presence of God in our daily lives. He doesn't step in just at the moment of a dramatic conversion and then withdraw for us to struggle as best we can. I've been in sick rooms and by the side of those who have had someone they loved die. I've sat with a woman whose reputation had just been ruined by a rumor that was being told about her. I've talked with teenagers who were convinced that their parents did not understand them—that they were left totally alone in this world, misunderstood and maltreated. Often I had no explanation as to why this sorrow had hit or how to right a tragic conflict. I've been at a loss for words except I could honestly assure the person I was addressing that the Spirit of God was with him, that the Risen Christ walked beside him. In these crisis situations I've never been alone. I'm more sure than ever that God is real; that God is Personal and loving; that God is concerned with you and me, and involved in all our lives.

Ten years after ordination my basic beliefs are strengthened.

But in the same period of time I've grown not so starry-eyed about the ministry. I suppose I thought when the Presbytery laid hands on my head I'd undergo some kind of metamorphosis. I didn't—and as I've come to know my fellow clergymen better I'm convinced they didn't either. One of the passages of scripture that had great weight in my decision to enter the ministry was the story of the call of the prophet Isaiah. You'll remember he was in the Temple praying when he had the vision of the Lord surrounded by seraphim who sang "holy, holy, holy." And when the Lord said, "Whom shall I send, and who will go for us?" the young Isaiah replied "Here I am. Send me." This is what I felt I was doing when I sought ordination. Only I forgot that the man who said this originally had just confessed that he had unclean lips and dwelt in the midst of a people of unclean lips. He was forgiven at that moment—but he would sin again, as we know in fact Isaiah did. And I now realize that I as a man commissioned by God to be His messenger am not and will not be perfect. I can be forgiven, but I'll always bear scars of former sins. And many times the sin will still be alive, for I will not have confessed. What I said earlier about all men failing short of the glory of God I now know applies to ministers, and to me. I have no illusions that the clergy are better than other Christians.

I know rather that some of us are perhaps worse off than our parishioners. We're all familiar with devoted physicians who neglect and ruin their own health through their service to other people. I've seen the same happen in the ministry. Men become so involved in teaching others that they have no time for relaxed study when they can recharge their own minds—so intellectually they die. Pastors give of their time to members of the flock, until there are not enough minutes left in the day to walk beside the still waters and refresh their own souls. So you find ordained ministers who lead others to the throne of grace, but whose own prayer life is withering from neglect. And this is true not only of private worship, but pubic too. Some of you consider it a duty and a chore to come to church each Sunday. Do you have any idea how fortunate you are? How I yearn for the privilege of being a part of the congregation on the Sundays of my vacation or when I go off to a conference. Can you imagine what it's like to get to go to church only three or four times a year? I've missed public worship these past nine years, for it's not the same when you're up here leading. I think the lack of corporate worship has left its mark on me—as it does on most other ministers. Perhaps all these deficiencies in us—in me—are part of what Christ meant when he said "he who would save his life will lose it, and he who loses his life for my sake will find it." I have lost, had to give up, some of the things in life I cherish most to serve you, the church to which I have been called. Yet perhaps this is part of the dying required of me if I would find my life in Christ.

Those times when I feel drained, when it seems to me that I'm not as alert intellectually as I was ten years ago, or as disciplined in the life of prayer, my mind goes back to the story in the 17th chapter of Exodus when Israel was doing battle with Amalek. Moses held up his hand to bless the children of Israel, and as long as he blessed them they prevailed. But his hands grew weary so that he could no longer do that which was needful—even that which he so much wanted to do. Then according to the story Aaron and Hur put a stone beneath his arm and upheld his hand for him until the sun went down. The story is a little bloodthirsty, but it illustrates wonderfully the way in which a man of God who grows weary in service needs support and strength from at least some of the people to whom he is sent as leader. Ten years ago I thought I could get all the strength I needed directly from God through my own worship and prayer life. Now I feel that is not true. For as I have already indicated, a faithful pastor has to sacrifice many opportunities for being refilled. Then he turns to his people and asks them to uphold him, as Moses asked Aaron and Hur to do. This I am asking of you. Feed me with ideas; press on me books and articles to read. Give me the privilege of participating in public prayer led by someone else. Don't always turn to me in committee meetings, but you lift our church to God in prayer and let me follow along and say "amen." And above all pray for me daily in your worship at home. This week at Ferncliff I taught a workshop on "Personal Spiritual Growth." When we came to intercessory prayer I asked the high school students how many of them prayed daily, or even weekly, for their pastor. Only one hand went up in a room of twenty-five—and she was the daughter of a minister. It makes me wonder how many of you are praying for me with regularity. I need it. I don't look at the ministry through rose colored glasses any more. I know we are sinful and weak in many ways—and I'm among the least of the saints. When my own prayer life is not enough, I need your encouragement, your supporting fellowship, your daily intercessions.

Now if my view of the ministry seems a bit disillusioned, my belief about the Church which we ministers serve is quite different. I know there is being a great deal said and written these days about the weakness and irrelevance of the Church. Many observers feel that decisions are being made, thought patterns being formulated, by the advertising men on Madison Avenue, or the egg-heads in Washington, or the Communists in Moscow—by just about every institution on earth except the Church, which they say sits on the sidelines moaning or applauding, but making no real impression. I think this is a wrong appraisal. The Church doesn't have as much money to spend as Madison Avenue, nor can it prepare studies such as come out of government agencies, nor can it use methods as brutally effective as those employed by the Communists. But the Church never has. It has always seemed hopelessly out numbered, shamefully weak. But so did the Church's Lord. He was roughed up and crucified—yet he triumphed in the end, while Rome and the Sanhedrin passed away into oblivion. Our culture will change. The present nations of the earth will disappear. Nuclear weapons will be outmoded. But the Church will remain, and will still be doing its work quietly yet effectively when all else is gone. Though I realize more and more how small my contribution will be, I am glad that I am devoting what talents and time I have to serve the world through the church instead of some other institution.

This does not mean the Church is perfect—that it is doing its work as it should be doing. It is full of flaws and sins. We are not preaching the "unsearchable riches of Christ," but too often just deal with superficialities. We are not revealing to "all men" the "plan of the mystery hidden for ages in God" but now revealed in Christ Jesus. We go to a few of our neighbors, if they are already our friends and make it easy for us to broach the subject. We don't go to "all men," but restrict ourselves to those of our social and economic and racial background. We don't go to "all men," but stay here in America where it's comfortable, and send just a pitiful handful of representatives abroad to the uncommitted nations of the world. And even when we do go, we often just talk without acting. Do we bind up the brokenhearted? Do we proclaim liberty to the captive people of this earth? Do we open the prison for those who are bound? No, the Church—the community which is the best hope for fulfilling God's will on earth—is timid and fearful and too selfish to turn loose of what it has for the welfare of someone else.

But still, despite all its imperfections, the Church is the best hope that I find. This increases the urgency of its setting its house in order, of its purging itself of imperfections, of its putting in positions of leadership the very best men and women of our day, the cream of the crop of the boys and girls who will set the pace in the next generation. One of the moving stories in the Acts of the Apostles tells of how Paul in a vision one night saw a young man who said, "Come over into Macedonia to help us." I wish many of you, many of your children, would see and hear that vision in our time. There is such a need in the world today. There are more spectacular ways of meeting the need, but I know of no more effective way than through full time work in Christ's Church. Jesus once said, "I tell you, lift up your eyes, and see how the fields are already white for harvest" (John 4:35), and again, "the harvest is plentiful, but the laborers are few." I am sure He would say the same thing today—is, as a matter of fact, saying it now through my lips. He is saying it to some of you who already have professions but who are not too old to change the sphere in which you work. He is saying it to some of you young people who are even now making vocational decisions. He is saying it to some of you parents of young children who can plant seeds that someday may bear fruit.

After ten years in the ministry I am basically filled with hope. I am more convinced than ever that the message we proclaim is true. I believe that as the Church has been the instrument of redemption in past ages, so it can be in the present and the future despite all its faults which are so apparent to a careful observer. I even have hopes for the ministry of the Church. I have taken clergymen down from the pedestal on which I once placed them. We are sinners. Many of us have run dry. Some of us do not have the support from our congregations that we need. But we are heirs of a promise. "The Spirit of the Lord is upon me, because the Lord has anointed me to bring good tidings to the afflicted." Some way, somehow, the Spirit and the power will come to His servants who enter this work. I believe that ten years from now He will still be upholding me. And I pray ten years from now I shall be joined in this work by a number of people from this congregation.

GOD'S SPIRIT CAN WORK WONDERS

Date: December 6, 1964—Second Sunday in Advent, Holy Communion

Lectionary: Psalm 148; Romans 9:1-8; **St. John 3:1-17**

Hymns: I do not have the bulletin for that Sunday so do not know what hymns were sung.

This sermon was preached one month after my wife, Ann, who suffered from depression, had become a patient at the Menninger Clinic in Topeka, Kansas. Prior that she had for two months been a patient at Arkansas Baptist Hospital. My sister and brother-in-law in Knoxville, Tennessee had, at the end of October, offered to take my three children to live with them while Ann was in Topeka. The congregation was aware of these developments in our family.

"Truly, truly, I say to you, unless one is born of water and the Spirit, he cannot enter the kingdom of God…Nicodemus said to him, 'How can this be?' Jesus answered him, 'Are you a teacher of Israel, and yet you do not understand this?'"

I had already been planning to preach this morning on the story of Nicodemus' visit with Jesus, but last night, about twelve, the direction of what I planned to say took a new turn. Gert Behanna, the author of *The Late Liz* for those of you who have not met her on her previous visits to Little Rock, was in town for an Episcopal youth convention and after it was over, Bishop and Mrs.

Brown most graciously allowed me to have the evening with her. By the way, she sent her warm love to you who came to know her this summer. Gert is a night-owl, and as many of you know I have nocturnal habits on Saturdays myself. We sat and talked into the wee hours in that frank and intimate way two people "in Christ" can converse, even though they have not seen each other for months. Some of you know what I mean. There is no chit-chat, there is no polite folderol. You ask questions that are on your heart, you share experiences and insights. This kind of conversation *can* go on at any hour of the day, but somehow it's easier in the middle of the night. It is no accident that the conversation between Nicodemus and Jesus took place in the evening.

Our Lord set the tone for this particular discussion when he said, "truly, truly, I say to you, unless one is born anew, he cannot see the kingdom of God." But Nicodemus didn't pick it up. He replied by asking how a grown man could enter his mother's womb a second time. Jesus tried again—"unless one is born of water and the Spirit," but the visitor still just didn't get it. Finally the Master, who was so wonderfully patient with those whose abilities were limited, exploded "Are you a teacher of Israel, and yet you do not understand this?" Scholars differ as to whether this was sarcasm, irony or just plain disgust. Nicodemus was a Pharisee, which meant he had devoted his whole life to carrying out the law in every detail. Obviously, therefore, he knew the Scriptures well. He was a member of the Sanhedrin, which meant that his life was closely tied to the worship in the Temple and all religious activities. He was a man of wealth who had access to cultural and educational advantages. There are some people who don't understand the truth because they are either immature or underprivileged. There are others who draw a blank because they don't *want* to comprehend. They don't want to grow and as a result have their way of life so revolutionized that no word but "re-born" can adequately describe it. They are happy to submit to the externals of religion, but they are scared to let the Spirit, the Spirit of power, get turned loose. They just stare back in blank amazement and say, "I don't know what you mean." This Jesus couldn't and wouldn't take. Nicodemus knew the writings of Jeremiah and Ezekiel where God had promised "a new spirit I will put within you" (Ezekiel 36:26). If he wanted to reject the offer of life that was one thing, but to plead lack of understanding is another.

Jesus said we must be born of "water and the Spirit." I take "water" to stand for the external parts of the religious life—the printed book called the Bible, the organization named the Church, the visible and tangible Sacraments, the celebration of seasons such as Christmas. Those of you who know me at all must realize I would be the last to disparage these concrete expressions of our faith. But I do know that sometimes we can get so wrapped up in them for their own sake that we forget they are just channels of God's grace, forms without meaning unless the Spirit is present. This was the trap into which Nicodemus fell. And sometimes it seems that the danger is more acute for those with the most advantages. Just as Nicodemus became so involved in carrying out the minute provisions of the law that he missed the prophet's promise of a new heart, so some of us who are most diligent in our study of the Bible are deafest of all when God speaks to us through it. We are so involved in keeping the kings of Israel in order we can't hear, or won't, His word of judgment or of hope. We who are officers become so distracted with the details of serving the bread and wine we fail to "feed on him in our hearts by faith with thanksgiving." The budget looms so big on the horizon we forget the Church is first of all the Body of Christ, subject to His will and sustained by His power. We make so much to-do about Christmas we overlook the miracle of God's presence in our midst. And the sad part of it is that often it is those of us who are the "church-iest" of all, the really good people and pillars of society—the Nicodemuses of 1964—who are most dense. The outward motions, the printed page, the "water" part we understand. But this business of being taken over by God's spirit makes us uneasy to say the least. I wonder if the Lord doesn't want to ask us, "Are you a teacher of Israel, a professing Christian, and yet you do not understand this?"

I wish you could have shared with me the hours with Gert Behanna last night as she told me some of her recent experiences. Here's a woman who has been born again, and is upheld by God's love day after day, and not only Gert but those she loves. Part of the spiritual life of course is prayer—and those who heard her talk will remember her older son Bill, called Alan in *The Late Liz*. For sixteen years she has been praying for him, and asking others to do the same. Nine years ago he quit drinking, but still he was bitter, lonely and empty. Gert told me last night in October, 1963, Bill had surgery for cancer of the throat, and amazingly enough the surgeon was able to spare his vocal cords. In August of this year, two days before Gert flew to Europe, Bill called from California to say there had been a recurrence. This time the doctor held out no hope of saving his voice—but miraculously again he was spared. A few weeks later Bill was so happy about his deliverance he went out and got drunk, fell out of a moving automobile and broke all his incisions open. He phoned Gert, who was in the middle of a three-week mission in Alabama, to come out to him, but his speech revealed he was still drinking and she turned him down flat. She said when he got in AA and reported back to the hospital to call her again, and she'd drop whatever she was doing. Three weeks passed and no word came at all. She did not know if he was sick on skid row or dying in a charity ward. Finally she called Bishop Pike to get him to send out a missing persons alert. The next morning at nine he phoned back to say Bill had been located in a half-way house for alcoholics attached to his own cathedral. Bill is in AA and sober. His incisions are re-healing, but far more important than that at the age of 46 he has for the first time since he was a boy been able to say "thank you" to his mother and mean it. He has thanked her for her firmness and thanked her for her prayers. The battle is not over, nor is all the suffering behind. But the Spirit of God has worked in wondrous ways again, this time in a man who seemed beyond all hope, except to a mother who had herself been reborn at fifty-three. Wherever the Spirit is allowed into someone's heart, amazing things do happen and the joy they come to know is contagious. Don't ever let yourself become so involved with the facts in Bible study, with the business of Church work, with the theories about Communion that you miss the Spirit who gives you new life and upholds you while you live it.

Let me add one further word of personal testimony about the role of the Spirit in the Christian life. Most of you know the strain under which I have lived the past few months with illness at home and the responsibilities attached to it. There were times there for a few weeks when I felt I was at the point of exploding or breaking myself. Because of my profession, attendance at church of course remained a necessity, but many other of the formal aspects of the Christian life fell by the wayside. Had they been all I had to lean upon, I would never have made it. But even at my lowest moment I remember having a sense of the presence of God's Spirit, guiding me as I made decisions, giving me physical strength to go on, enabling me to have patience in dealing with people when I was tempted to snap back. Of course I was not alone in opening my heart to the Spirit. Many of you, and dozens of other friends, were praying for me. I do not know *how* prayer works nor how the Spirit does. As Jesus told Nicodemus, the movements of the spirit are as mysterious as those of the wind. But intercessory prayer and the outpouring of the Spirit seem to be related. This was true in the life of Gert's son, Bill. It was true in my own life. I came through some dark weeks with a calm confidence in God. I emerged from them not bitter, but profoundly grateful. I feel not alone, but more surrounded by friends and love than ever before in my life. I have learned so much the last few months. I hope I am a bigger and deeper person—and I think I am. If so this is not of my own doing. Any growth I have experienced is the result of God's loving and powerful Spirit.

Do you know His presence in your own life? It doesn't make any difference how regular you are at church, or how much you may know about the Bible—until the Spirit pours into you, and takes over from you, you have not yet been re-born, you have not yet entered the Kingdom of God. If you have not yet had this experience, which need not be dramatic to be powerfully real, pray for this grace today. And if you have, speak out in witness and let others know that beyond and above and below the outward forms there is a life wonderful beyond all describing. This life Jesus wanted for Nicodemus. This life—which Gert exemplifies, which Bill perhaps has begin to know, which I have had confirmed—I want for you. "Truly, truly I say to you, unless one is born of water and the Spirit, he cannot enter the kingdom of God."

CHRIST CAN BRING PEACE AND JOY

Date: March 21, 1965—Third Sunday in Lent

Lectionary: Psalm 51; **Romans 5:1-11**; St. Luke 4:51-62

Hymns: "Rejoice, Ye Pure In Heart," "They Cast Their Nets In
   Galilee," "God, Be Merciful To Me"

*In the 1998 fire in my apartment the notebook containing my sermons
between June 13 and November 28, 1965 were destroyed, so the variety
from which to select one sample sermon for that year is limited.*

"Since, therefore, we are now justified by his blood, much more
shall we be saved by him from the wrath of God."

Some of you present this morning may remember that last
Sunday I preached on the beginnings of the Christian life, what St.
Paul calls justification. In calling for an evangelistic witness from
you, I described the bare bones of the Gospel as including a reminder
of men's sin, news of God's gracious offer to treat us as though we
were something more, and a challenge to accept this through faith.
Today I want to move on from the beach-head to further explo-
rations. This past week most of us have been excited again by the
advances being made in space travel. It's not going to be too long
before somebody's going to land on the moon. Now if his ship finds
a safe spot to light, won't you be terribly disappointed if he just takes
a picture to prove he was there, and then heads back home without
getting out and looking around? Well, for a sinner like you or me to

shout "Hurray! God's washed my slate clean" and then to fail to follow up to see what other experiences can yet be found, would be equally distressing. And as a matter of a fact, the reason most of us have so few opportunities to tell another person how to establish contact with God in Christ is that we bring back such meager and hazy reports as to what life in Him can be like that no one inquires. There's a lot of interest right now in getting to the moon, but you know as well as I, once the feat has been achieved and repeated two or three times by the curious, nobody's going to spend the money and time required getting to that celestial body unless the pioneers report something they find there of value—mineral riches, or beauty, or strategic military bases. Certainly there has been no mass movement of people up the sides of Mt. Everest since this tallest of mountains was finally scaled, for there's nothing up there on the peak. Maybe more people would ask you and me how to *enter* the Christian life if we could display in our behavior as well as proclaim through our lips the fact that it *is* a glorious kingdom in which to live. St. Paul tells the Romans of two characteristics of this realm which he had discovered and sampled that he found good.

The first mark of the new life which he lists is *peace*. "Therefore, since we are justified by faith we have peace…" Now we must always remember in the New Testament peace does not mean tranquility and ease. In the words of the hymn we just sang, "The peace of God, it is no peace, But strife closed in the sod." When Jesus said, "Peace I leave with you, my peace I give to you" he distinguished it carefully from what the world puts in its place and tries to pass off as a satisfactory substitute. He was in an upper room in Jerusalem, eating for the last time with the twelve disciples and about to go out to His betrayal and crucifixion when He said, "peace I leave with you." Let's get straight right off that we're not talking about undisturbed slumber or daylight hours of restful solitude. It's much deeper than that.

"Since we are justified by faith, we have peace…with *God*." This, of course, is the prerequisite for any other peace. Until we are justified it cannot exist, for in our natural state we are enemies of God, men who have rebelled and are trying to overthrow the rightful King. Jesus taught us that even when we are fighting Him hardest, God still loves us—but we're not at peace; any more than there is peace in a family at the moment the disobedient child is forcing his father to spank him, or his mother to strip him of all privileges. There is parental love all along, but strife is also present. And this is the way we are related to God—until we do the things I outlined last week—acknowledge ourselves as sinners, accept His offer of reconciliation. It may be bitterly hard to pray "For I know my transgressions, and my sin is ever before me." But for one who, believing that God really is like Jesus in understanding and mercy can confess this honestly, there does come an inner peace. "The strife is o'er, the battle done." Those who live the Christian life at times, of course, stray away from God for a while; and do things which offend Him. But these are no more than border clashes compared with a full-fledged war. Never do we, who live in Christ, have to be afraid of God. Never again do we ask whether He is *for* us or *against* us. We who have surrendered to Him know He is our friend, and we are at peace.

This therefore, probably for the first time, enables us to be at peace with ourselves. Of course the most perfect example ever offered of One who had come to terms with Himself was Jesus. "When the days drew near for him to be received up, he set his face to go to Jerusalem." If Jesus was really human, as I believe, He did not know in detail all that awaited Him. But it would have been clear to anyone as discerning as He that the forces of evil were gathering against Him. I doubt that he anticipated just when or how the end would come, but I'm sure that as He left Galilee He realized He would never return—in this life. Yet the picture we get of Jesus moving toward Jerusalem is one of a man at peace with Himself. For a brief while in Gethsemane, because He was human, there was a struggle—then the calm returned. To see your whole life work ridiculed and rejected; to see friends desert you; to undergo the torments of crucifixion—and still to have an inner peace—this is a miracle. This is a wonder, a mystery. Yet Jesus had

94

it. And those who have lived through Him and with Him have displayed it. They have not always approved of the way there were treated outwardly; often their ignominious defeat, their early death, was not what they would have chosen. Nobody would expect a young girl to want to be tied to a stake to be burned. A man, taking a stand for what he thinks is right, doesn't want to be hit on the head by a hoodlum—though he knows in advance it might happen. But as the flames lick around the young girl's feet or the blood flows from the man's head, they can know Christian peace. This peace with one's self comes from turning over life and fame and fortune to a God who is a Friend. St. Paul knew this as he awaited trial and beheading. Some of us perhaps know peace with ourselves under less dramatic circumstances.

And the man who is a peace with God and self can then be at peace with neighbors. Once more this does not mean indiscriminately approving whatever anyone says or does. Jesus on his way to Jerusalem rebuked James and John; He called the hands of three men who sought to become His disciples because they were superficial. But he didn't hate any of them, though He saw through what they said and did. He loved *them*, though not their deeds. And he also loved the Samaritans who rudely refused His band a place of shelter and some food while they travelled. The kind of peace which enables a man to turn the other cheek and pray for those who are his enemies is a mystery. It's a miracle. It comes by grace, as a gift from God. We never have a right to it—but it is one of the things those who enter the Christian life can look forward to discovering.

Salvation includes peace. Secondly, it includes joy. Even in the Old Testament there is a wonderful note of rejoicing. I was struck, as I studied the 51st Psalm, the great Penitential Psalm of confession, how often even here the note is sounded—"fill me with joy and gladness…let the bones which thou hast broken rejoice…restore to me the joy of thy salvation." And when we move to the New Testament the mood becomes even more exhilarated and exhilarating. On the day of Pentecost the followers of Jesus became so ecstatic that they were accused of being drunk on new wine. Paul and Silas, in jail in Philippi, got so wound up singing hymns that they kept all their fellow prisoners awake until past midnight. You've often heard me repeat the epigram, "Presbyterianism is that which cannot keep one from sinning but can take all the joy out of doing it." Of course this is not only amusing, but a terrible condemnation of us. In so far as it is true, it means we have missed both the power and the joy of the Gospel—and perhaps the latter of them is the greater loss. This remark is made of us because we are sometimes dour and ponderous. But even our Calvinistic ancestors knew better than this. In the Shorter Catechism they wrote, in answer to the question, "What is man's chief end?" the reply, "To glorify God and enjoy Him forever." Remember that word "enjoy," and know that in so far as you mature in the Christian life, it will become more and more a part of your vocabulary.

In good Calvinistic manner, we begin by enjoying God Himself. I wonder how many of you ever pause to check the dominant emotion within you when you close the bedroom door for a period of private prayer; when you find fifteen minutes to read the Bible; when you get up in the morning and realize it is Sunday with its opportunity for sharing in public worship? Do you sigh, suggesting this contact with God is a burden to be borne? Do you cringe in fear, as you would upon entering the presence of someone you don't trust? Are your bored? Are you confused and mystified? Or does your cup overflow with joy, the way it does when you spend the evening with a friend you cherish; the way it does down at the airport when the plane door opens and you see a loved one from whom you have been separated too long? Does it ever occur to you that you can *enjoy* God, "have fun" might not be too strong a term to use? The experience of those who have travelled far down the Christian way is that this pleasure is a normal part of their daily life. This doesn't mean we have to drag Him down to our level. But after all, when Someone knows you intimately, cares for you even when you're at your worst, seeks your best interests, and is Himself wondrously wise and strong—is it not proper to look forward with longing to fellowship with Him? Christian people enjoy their God.

They also enjoy His creation. It's clear in the Gospel stories that Jesus took great pleasure in the world about Him. He commented on the beauty of the lilies. He found food good to eat, and to the dismay of prohibitionists ever since, wine good to drink. St. Francis of Assisi is often regarded as the most Christ-like of all those who have been canonized by the Roman Catholic Church. You'll remember how he spoke of Brother Sun and Sister Moon, and he talked with the birds and animals. Gert Behanna tells how prior to her conversion, though there were acres of garden and a couple of hothouses on her estate, she never was aware of any flower until it was cut and put in a vase. Then shortly after her dramatic about-face, when she went out to the California desert to think, she suddenly became aware of how good sand feels when you run it through your fingers; how graceful a lizard can be sliding in and out of rocks; how sweet is the perfume of a wild flower. She said she began to think she was off her rocker. Not long after that, on a trip to New Haven, she met Mr. Latourette, the professor at Yale who has meant so much to me. She said immediately she recognized in his face and conversation the marks of Christ, so she got him off in the corner and told him about how she liked to feel the dirt and smell the flowers; and she asked, "Am I crazy?" She said she'll never forget the way he threw back his head and laughed and said, "Of course not. Anyone who comes to know God well is bound to enjoy the work of His hands. And the closer you grow to Him the more pleasure you'll find."

Then St. Paul throws in joy on another plane. "More than that, we rejoice in our sufferings." The psychiatrists might have a field-day with this, labeling it as masochism. But if they would take time really to know the Apostle, they'd find he didn't get any kick out of hurting for hurting's sake. The Greek here means, literally, not suffering but "pressures." And they take on significance only because they could help produce what the RSV calls "enduring" but that's a bad translation too. He has in mind not a quality of patient endurance, but an active conquest. Fortitude might be better. And this finds its meaning in the "character" which can emerge from it. Again the Greek word is the one used for metal which has been put in a furnace and had all the impurities removed. "Sterling," like in silver, would be our equivalent. St. Paul found even the pressures of imprisonment, financial hardship, impending death were causes for joy—because, in Christ, they no longer got him down as once they would have. They simply purged him, and freed him, of lesser concerns. The more his outward situation deteriorated, the more he became filled with hope. So of course he rejoiced in his sufferings. And many like him ever since have known joy in situations which to the outsider seemed undiluted disaster.

There are so many other qualities, fruits of the Spirit, to be found in the Christian journey. There's patience and there's courage and there's hope. But today let's remember especially the gifts of peace and joy that come to those who live in Christ. Confessing sins, acceptance in faith of reconciliation or pardon, are essential. People who do not believe need to know about them. But there is so much more than just being justified. We go on for the rest of our lives, for the rest of eternity "being saved." It is not something that happened once and then is over. We grow, in breadth and height and depth. If we are not effective as evangelists, perhaps it's not that we are lacking something to *say*—it's that there is so little *radiance* about us that no one comes to us with questions, wondering why. For who would seek guidance on the secret of life from one whose life is not full? So perhaps the place for us, who are professing Christians but ineffective evangelists, to begin is with a prayer that our lives may be filled with gifts of the spirit—perhaps, especially, the gifts of peace and joy. We ask these not only for our own sake, but also that we may be of greater service.

Breaking Down Barriers

Date: January 9, 1966—First Sunday after Epiphany

Lectionary: Psalm 72; **Ephesians 3:1-13**; **St. Matthew 2:1-12**

Hymns: I do not have the bulletin for that Sunday so do not
   know what hymns were sung.

*At the start of 1966 Lyndon Johnson's Great Society push was in full
swing with the passage of the Civil Rights Acts of 1964 and 1965 and
the War on Poverty. It was a time of change and optimism. The war in
Vietnam had not yet taken its toll.*

"Behold, wise men from the East came to Jerusalem, saying
'Where is he who as been born king of the Jews? For we
have seen his star in the East, and have come to worship him.'"
And from St. Paul's Letter to the Ephesians, "…you can perceive
my insight into the mystery of Christ…that is, how the Gentiles
are fellow heirs, members of the same body, and partakers of the
promise in Christ Jesus through the gospel."

I had just about persuaded myself that there wasn't any need
of preaching to you this Sunday on the meaning of Epiphany, nor
even to touch on the story of the Wise Men, for I hate to bore people by repeating information they already know and hammering
away at insights they have long ago accepted. But just as I was
coming to this conclusion I called in the hospital on an out-of-
town Presbyterian family who said on the night before they had

asked the priest who serves as chaplain why in the world the sisters at St. Vincent's hadn't taken their Christmas decorations down since New Year's was over. He explained to them that in the Church's calendar, as distinct from the merchants', the season of Christmas does not begin until Christmas Eve and it lasts for twelve days, until January 6 when, according to tradition, the Wise Men reached Bethlehem. My friends said, "He called January 6 'Ep-i-*fany*' or some such word." I replied, "It's pronounced 'Epiphany,' and we Presbyterians celebrate it too—or at least we do at Grace Church." The wife then exclaimed, "Oh, I guess we do too. I've seen 'First Sunday after Epiphany' at the top of the bulletin, but I never quite understood what it meant." Now this couple are active and faithful Presbyterians of many years' standing. I decided right then if they didn't know, probably a good many of you don't either. So here goes.

The significance of the Wise Men, or magi, is that they were Gentiles, from a great distance, and were not only practitioners but leaders in a pagan religion. As so often happens, the more research I did on the subject of the magi the less certain I became of precisely who they were or what they did. You know, usually the only people who can give you a cut and dried answer to most questions are those whose information is limited and whose understanding is superficial. The closer we get to truth the more aware we grow of its complexity and vastness. But let's get back to the magi. In origin they may have been one of the native tribes in Media when the Aryan invaders swept down from the north who, after resisting awhile, decided "If you can't lick 'em, jine 'em." By the time Herodotus, the Greek historian, wrote about 400 B.C. they had become the priestly caste within the Persian Empire, very similar to the Levites within Judaism. The religion of that area became Zoroastrianism. No sacrifice could be made without at least one of the magi present. But they went beyond the ritual to become students of philosophy and natural science, especially astronomy. They gained such power of influence over the rulers of Persia that about 300 years after the birth of Jesus they were able to engineer a bloody persecution of both Jews and Christians living in that land. Now apparently it was some of these priests and scholars who came looking for the king of the Jews.

We are always impressed when people travel a long way on a pilgrimage. Often at a reunion or homecoming ceremony, a prize is given to the one who travelled the greatest number of miles to get there. It also intrigues us when folk arrive in exotic dress. I remember when watching Queen Elizabeth II's coronation the show was almost stolen by the 350 pound Queen of Tonga who came up from the South Pacific in native garb. But we miss the real point unless we realize that these pagans—not back-sliding members of their religion who didn't really care one way or the other, but theologians and priests—were, in their desire for fellowship with God, turned to the Jews. And even more startling, a faithful Jewish family who sought in every way to fulfill the law, allowed them to enter their home, accepted their gifts, and raised no protest when they worshipped the child. Only when we recall the violent contempt and hatred Jews and Gentiles felt for each other at this point in history can we begin to grasp the revolutionary significance of the Wise Men story. A Jewish home into which a Gentile entered was considered unclean and its inhabitants had to submit themselves to all kinds of acts of ritual purification. A dish touched by a Gentile was hopelessly polluted and simply had to be broken. We are not told what Mary and Joseph did with the gold and frankincense and myrrh. Presumably they accepted them. But if so, they violated a taboo; they broke down a wall that was high and thick. William Barclay says that the basic sin of the ancient world was contempt—mutual contempt which kept men apart from each other, and therefore at a distance from God. In the house in Bethlehem this solid barrier cracked. The first shaft of light pierced the thick blanket of clouds. St. Matthew's story puts in dramatic form good news St. Paul stated in more theological terms.

First of all, the Apostle wrote that he had been given an insight into the mystery of Christ, "that…the Gentiles are fellow heirs, members of the same body, partakers of the promise." In the

Greek it is even more striking for the three nouns are "co-heirs, co-members, co-sharers." Obviously it was hard for men of that day to grasp this truth, else St. Paul would not have had to devote such a large part of his ministry to defending it. This seems somewhat surprising since at least some traces of appreciation for God's love of all men can be found in the Old Testament. The Book of Jonah was written to say God cares not just for the Jews but for all men, even the citizens of the wicked city of Nineveh. The last 26 chapters of Isaiah, often called II Isaiah, speak of nations coming to the light of the glory of God. Psalm 72 which we read this morning looks toward the day when the King will reign over the whole earth. There is a universalism in the Old Testament which was almost forgotten by nationalistic and over-patriotic Jews. But even at its height, the Old Testament tells of Gentiles coming into the Lord's fold only by submitting to the Law, and worshipping at the Temple—that is, by becoming Jews. There was a place for proselytizing, for conversion—but not for a free acceptance of men on a new basis. This was unheard of until the birth of Jesus.

The treatment of the magi in Bethlehem; Jesus' willingness to sit at table with publicans and sinners; Peter's readiness to baptize the Roman soldier Cornelius and his household; Paul's throwing open the doors of the Church to Gentiles in every city—these things were radically new. They never denied that the Jews were God's people. They simply added that the heathen, the Gentiles, could be too if they would simply believe. So the arms of God, which at first seemed to protect only Abraham and his descendants; which then were seen to open up to men of all races provided they submitted to the Jewish Law; are now beheld as thrown back, stretched wide, not only *permitting* men to His embrace but *beckoning* them, *inviting* them, *pleading* with them.

The circle of God's love is like the ripple caused when a rock dropped into a calm body of water keeps on growing wider and wider. The history of the church, at least in its purer ages, is the history of the inclusion of more and more people, of the welcome of more and more types, into the household of faith. Those of you

studying church history in church school have already read of some
of the geographical extension of missionary labors—to the west as
far as Britain, to the north into Russia, to the south across Africa
and down into Ethiopia, to the east perhaps as far as India. Soon
you'll come to the expansion of Catholicism when the Americas
were discovered, and a practical way of getting to Asia and Africa.
Then in the last century Protestant missions came into their own
so that now there is hardly any territory left on the face of this
globe without at least a Christian bridgehead established.

This geographical expansion having run its course, the
Church then began pioneering in new ways. The barrier of color
that has separated men from men, and Christian brothers within
the Church itself, was attacked. It is this that we have been caught
up in these last fifteen years. The struggle has been bitter at times,
but the war is won. There are still costly mopping up operations
ahead of us, but the point has been made in a way that can never
be reversed, that white and black and yellow men are co-heirs, co-
members, co-sharers of the promise in Christ Jesus. Now already,
while we in our part of the country are still having difficulty ad-
justing to this last enlargement of the concept of Christian brotherhood, the creative spirits in the Church seem to be advancing
on a new front. They are forcing us to face up to the fact that while
even the writer of Psalm 72 sang, "he delivers the needy when he
calls, the poor and him who has no helper"; while Jesus included
in the defense of His ministry the statement "the poor have good
news preached to them"; while the early Church included many
slaves and former criminals—the Church in our day is largely a
middle class institution, a haven for the comfortable and the affluent. Some of us feel poor because we can't have all the luxuries
we might like. But there are not many people in the Presbyterian
Church who come to church hungry because they can't afford
breakfast. There are not many who come in bare feet. There may
be a few more Baptists or Catholics or Pentecostals or Russian
Orthodox who come out of absolute poverty. But survey the ranks
of Christendom around the world and you'll find the percentage

very small. And surely it's not because there are no poor to be in-vited. With half to two-thirds of the world's population going to bed hungry every night, dare we turn our back and say we've done all we can do? The numbers of those in need is greater across the seas, but some exist right here in our own affluent society. There are people benefiting not in the least from the prosperity of our economy—who in fact, because of inflation, are worse off than be-fore. There are old people on small pensions; there are thousands trapped in the slums of the cities; there are rural slums in the mountains, on worn out farms, in the tenant house of plantations. These people have been forgotten by the Church—especially by the Presbyterian Church which with a shrug of the shoulders, and a wrinkle of the nose, says "They aren't our kind of folks." The new frontier of missionary work in the years ahead, I believe, will be in reaching out to, including, and assisting the poor whom our Lord loved so much, and among whom He chose to dwell. A new ripple is appearing on the surface of the water. It's very much like the wave that washed away the barrier between Jew and Gentile, that spread across continents in the missionary movement, that is still eating away the remains of the wall that separated black and white.

There's a second point St. Paul makes that you might find of great discomfort. "For this reason I, Paul, a prisoner for Christ Jesus on behalf of your Gentiles…" The Epistle was written from a jail in Rome. Paul was in chains because in espousing the cause of the Gentiles he had brought on himself the wrath of most of his fellow Jews. He warns us here that every time the concept of the Gospel is enlarged, every time the brotherhood of the faith is made more inclusive, opposition will arise. Sometimes it comes from outside the Church, from those who resent the fact that an invitation is extended to them. Just as the people of Jerusalem over whom Jesus wept turned against Him and cried, "Crucify him, crucify him," so history is full of examples of Muslims and Hindus and head-hunters in New Guinea who have attacked and killed missionaries sent to them. St. Vincent de Paul, when he established an order of nuns in Paris to work among the desperately poor, warned them "You must love them enough to enable them to forgive you for coming to their aid." But just as frequently, and more painfully, the opposition comes from *within*. It was not the Zoroastrians of Persia or the Greek worshippers of Zeus who dried up the missionary movement within Judaism, but the priests and the scribes who refused to make way for the spirit of God. The greatest handicap to the world mission enterprise has not been the hostility of Islam, but the lethargy and stinginess of professing Christians. The last bastion of racial segregation in this country apparently is going to be the Protestant Christian Church. Opposition to change, to enlargement, is found to come from without and within. So we are warned in Scripture.

But St Paul writes his friends, "not to lose heart over what I am suffering for you, which is your glory." He simply considered this part of the price that had to be paid. When old friends turned against him, when his arguments were distorted and misrepresented, when doors were closed to him, and finally his life was put in jeopardy—he did not fall prey to self pity; he did not grow resentful; he rejoiced and sang instead. He was so firmly convinced that he was doing the will of God in offering the gospel to an outcaste group that he did not even think of himself as being a prisoner of the Romans, but a prisoner of Christ. His chains were not a mark of shame, but a badge of honor. And so we should regard opposition which comes to us if it results not from stupidity or arrogance, but from the scandalous nature of the Gospel. The visit of the Wise Men brought on the massacre of the children of Bethlehem. Opening a new door will always make somebody mad.

And now a third thing I must bring you from this passage of scripture. "When you read this you can perceive my insight into the mystery of Christ, which was not made known to the sons of men in other generations as it has now been revealed…" The wisdom of God is greater than any human mind, and the love of God vaster than all our hearts put together. He does not reveal His whole purpose or strategy at one time, for we could not grasp it. Instead, He makes known His mystery bit by bit as we are ready for it. This is not to say that the purpose of God is incomplete. St. Paul writes in the next paragraph of "the plan for the mystery hidden for ages in God who created all things." But just as a mathematics teacher who understands trigonometry and calculus begins her grade school pupils with simple problems of adding two plus two, then moves into multiplication and on into division, so God in His mercy has done with us. There is a progression, not in the nature of God or in the quality of His love, but in the extent to which He reveals His mystery. There was a time when He offered His love to all the nations, and agreed to let them come through the door of Judaism. When the time was ripe, in Christ Jesus, He threw open a wider door of faith. In later times He has opened a whole succession of doors—through the Age of Discovery, the whole area of world missions; through Wilberforce, the conquest of human slavery; in our time, the rise above color consciousness; if I'm right in my prediction, in the years ahead, in redeeming the lot of the poor and the offering to them of real fellowship. What lies beyond that, I have no idea. We are like soldiers involved in a mighty battle. The supreme commander has a long range strategy, but the troops are given tactical assignments only a week or a day at a time. St. Paul writes of "the principalities and powers in the heavenly places" as being included in God's plan. I don't pretend to know what these terms mean—except they stand in my mind for the unknown. If I live to be seventy or eighty years old, I'm sure God will have the Church doing work, and attacking problems, I'm not even aware of. I just hope I don't fall victim to the snare of believing that the goals set during my youth are the final goals. This temptation comes to us all as we grow older. Someone has said "No one is more reactionary than a liberal dreamer whose dreams have all been fulfilled." The inclusiveness of God's love will never reach an outside limit. When I'm an old man, and you are old too, He'll be opening new doors and inviting in new aspects of His creation.

This is what the visit of the Wise Men stands for. This is what the word Epiphany means—the sending forth of the light, to Gentiles, to the dark continents, to men of all colors, to the poor, and to whoever or whatever remains in all creation. Let us pray that we may grow in our ability to understand and our willingness to serve rapidly enough to keep pace with God's revealing of His mystery.

Do You Want to Revert to the Way It Was Before He Came?

Date: August 20, 1967—13th Sunday after Trinity

Lectionary: Psalm 145; **I Samuel 3:1-18**; I Timothy 1:12-20

Hymns: "Sing Praise To God Who Reigns Above," "God Of The Prophets," "Be Thou My Vision"

This sermon was preached six weeks after David Graybill (the first of eventually thirteen interns at Grace Church) began his internship.

> *"And the word of the Lord was rare in those days; there was no frequent vision... Then the Lord called, 'Samuel! Samuel! And he said, 'Here I am!'"*

Cultures and nations go through cycles, and so do churches. Our text is describing Israel both as a religion and a political unit when it says "and the word of the Lord was rare in those days; there was no frequent vision." It had come to the end of an era known as that of the Judges, the time between the invasion of Palestine under Joshua and the crowning of Saul, the first king. According to tradition this period lasted four hundred years. During that time there were no leaders of the stature of Joshua or Moses. Only two insignificant prophets are referred to in the history of four centuries. There were no great generals; no statesman who could weld the loose confederation of twelve tribes into one strong force. It was not a time of great catastrophe. There had been minor defeats, but then there were occasional victories too. Israel was just in the doldrums. Its condition was symbolized by Eli the priest at Shiloh whose old age affected his eyes so that he could not see clearly, and so drained him of strength that he had lost control of his two sons who were serving under him. They were stealing meat which was meant to be sacrificed to God, and they were seducing women who came to the tent of meeting. Eli was aware of their misbehavior, but could not make himself do anything about it. The spiritual life of Israel, as well as its political condition, was at pretty low ebb.

It was at this point, when few expected to hear from the Lord any word or even to see visions again, that He chose to speak. "Then the Lord called, 'Samuel! Samuel!'" We are not sure how old Eli's companion was. The Hebrew word used of him, "young man" could be applied to people from birth to forty. Josephus, the Jewish historian, claims he was twelve, but we have no way of knowing. However it is clear that, compared to Eli, he was youthful. And not only was he immature in years. We're told Samuel did not *know* the Lord. He was still a child in the faith, with a lot of growing up to do. But he did come from a devout home. He had been dedicated to the Lord's work while a baby. He was being nurtured in the tent of meeting, serving in whatever limited ways he could, so he was in the right place at the right time. Then one night this young man, who had grown up in an era when no one really looked for a word to come from the Lord, was wakened from his sleep by the sound of someone calling him by name. It's clear he was not just projecting some inner desire, for three times he reported to Eli, thinking the old priest had called to him for help.

It become even more obvious this was no wishful dream once young Samuel realized Who it was addressing him. For the content of the message was so fearful the Lord said it would "make the two ears of every one that hears it… tingle" He was warned that his teacher and patron, Eli, and his whole household, were about to be punished for the blasphemy which his sons had committed, and of which the old priest had been aware. The message given Samuel was not a warning, a call to change even now. It was too late for that. He was to be, so to speak, not the public health worker warning of the danger of smoking, but the pathologist looking up from his slides and signaling to the surgeon just to sew the patient back up for it is too late to do any good. It's strange how often the true prophets whom God has called into His service have had to begin with a message of doom. When Isaiah had his vision in the Temple, the seraphim said "Go, and say to this people: 'Hear and hear, but do not understand; see and see, but do not perceive…until cities lie waste without inhabitant, and houses without men, and the land is utterly desolate." John the Baptist attacked the Scribes and Pharisees who came to be baptized saying "You brood of vipers! Who warned you to flee form the wrath to come?" The word which came to Samuel was no more pleasant. We can imagine why, the next morning, he was afraid to share his vision with Eli.

And here we discover a hidden hero in our story. For all of his faults—despite his connivance with the misdeeds of his sons, his general spiritual lethargy—Eli was the one who realized what was happening that night. He was not himself in close enough harmony with God to be the spokesman. But he did sense that the Lord was breaking through a blanket of silence, like a ray of sunshine piercing a layer of smog. Eli alerted Samuel to listen and respond, and identified for him the source of the vision. Then the next morning he insisted that the young man tell him what had been revealed. The fear in his assistant's eyes, his hesitancy to speak must have been warnings that it was bad news. It would have been easy for Eli not to press. He could have changed the subject or wandered off to eat. But he had courage enough to want to know the truth, however painful it might be. Then when the blow fell, when the sentence was pronounced on him and his household, he took it like a man. "It is the Lord; let him do what seems good to him." Eli may have failed in many other ways, but he was no coward. And he refused to live in a never-never world, a dream-land made up of phantasies, believing that whatever he wanted would come about simply because he desired it. He could, at several points, by failure to fulfill his role, have kept Samuel from being the channel of God's grace. He has never received top billing as the star of the play, but without his contribution the plot would not have progressed.

Samuel and Eli both had their roles to fill. And because they did, Israel suddenly began to be lifted up out of the doldrums. It was like a person recovering from depression. The deep valley and the monotonous plateaus began to give way to soaring mountains. The golden age of Israel began to dawn. Politically, the tribes became one nation. Under David and Solomon culture flourished. Samuel was followed by a whole series of prophets who brought religion to a high point never exceeded until the coming of Jesus. This episode which tells what happened to a young lad one night as he slept next door to the priest at Shiloh marks the beginning of a new era, the rebirth of a people and a church.

Now I was struck, as I read this passage, by how very relevant it is to our own situation. It seems to me once more "the word of the Lord is rare in our days; there is no frequent vision." I have an idea historians will look back on the late 1960s as not much more glorious in American annals than the late 1860s. Wherever you stand on the political spectrum, left-right-or-center, life in our nation probably seems to you to be in something of a slump. Neither hawks nor the doves are happy with the way things are going in Viet Nam. Religiously speaking the church boom is over and everybody knows it. And here in Grace church we seem to have slowed down from a full and joyful canter to a dog-trot. The exodus of so many of our strongest leaders to other cities has taken a toll. We are not falling apart at the seams, but we are not in a condition of ferment and excitement as we have been many times in the past. Some of our old stalwart leaders are tired, and new ones have not yet appeared to take their places.

Into this environment I believe the Lord has sent His word again. I don't want to overdraw the parallel—and I certainly realize it could be done. But I believe the Lord may be speaking to us in our day through another young man serving in the church, even as He spoke to and through Samuel long ago. I am deliberately preaching this sermon today while David Graybill is out of town supplying for a pastor on vacation, because knowing him I'm sure it would be a source of great embarrassment if he had to sit here in this chancel while I preach it. But there are some things which I feel led to say *about him* and his ministry, and *to you* concerning your response to him. When I came back from vacation—as a matter of fact, before it was even over—I began to get reports of strong reactions to the sermons David preached and the worship services he conducted during my absence. Some were very favorable, some extremely negative—or so I was told. I was warned that my phone would ring off the wall as soon as I returned to the study. But the calls never came. Apparently there has been a good bit of talking—but practically none of it to me, and even less directly to David to whom remarks should be addressed first of all.

There are four things I want to say.

The first is that I am firmly convinced David is in communion, or conversation if you will, with our Father who is in heaven. Apparently in one sermon he said something about not being sure who Jesus Christ was. On certain points about the nature of Christ he and I have real differences—healthy ones, I believe. I may be more orthodox than he in my Christology, but there are lots of areas where I have to confess that I just don't know. As a matter of fact, it's hard for me to imagine anyone who is intellectually and spiritually alive who does not have some doubts. Growth means change, and change leaves uncertainty. It's only when rigor mortis sets in that everything stays in place. David's young, and I for one am delighted he is probing and asking questions. Remember, Samuel was young too. And it was said of him at the time of his call, that he didn't even "know the Lord." Well, David does that. He and I try to have prayer together first thing in the morning of each working day. As I said last week, you really get to know another person when you share in his prayer life. I would not violate his confidence by divulging to anyone the contents of David's prayers. But I would like for you to know how very much he has grown since a year ago last June when we first met. When he returned to Yale from Little Rock last year, he sought out Kenneth Scott Latourette, the retired professor of missions who has meant so much to me, who has visited here at Grace Church. His students call him "Uncle Ken." There is probably no greater master of the devotional life in the Protestant world than Uncle Ken. He and David met weekly for prayer all last year. David learned and grew. So when he preaches, know you are sitting at the foot of one who speaks to and listens to the Lord most earnestly. He doesn't look pious—thank goodness; and he isn't, in the bad sense of that word. But he is a man who is truly open to what the Lord has to say. If Samuel were to come back, you'd all wait with bated breath to hear what message he might bring. Realize God can use our young man as a channel too.

Second, I'm told some of you did not like some of the things David said in his sermons—especially about Viet Nam. Well, I wasn't here and I don't know what, specifically, he did say. But I do know from the Bible's reports of the preaching of the prophets across many centuries, the people rarely enjoyed what they had to say. In those days the only preachers who always kept their congregations happy turned out later to be false prophets who for a price would say anything requested. The real test of preaching is not whether it is pleasing, but whether it is true. And the truth nearly always hurts. Now if you accept my word that David is a man of prayer who gives God a chance to speak to him, then I should think it would behoove you to listen to whatever message he brings back, to see if there is not something in it which you need to hear. This is not to say he is infallible. If I thought he were I sure wouldn't disagree with him on as many points as I do! But as Gamaliel said of the preaching of Peter and the apostles, if it is of men it will prove wrong, if it is of God, you won't be able to overthrow it, and you might even be found opposing God. Wait a little while. Time has a way of testing many things. If he is wrong—or rather, to the *extent* he is wrong (for we are all wrong a good part

113

of the time) that will become apparent. You can, and should sort out the wheat from the chaff. But don't assume that everything which tastes unpleasant is necessarily chaff. Eli was prepared to hear the truth from Samuel even though it was a bitter message of doom for him and his family. I hope you will remain equally open.

Third, David can not only help you, but you have an opportunity to be of such wonderful service to him. I've already said Eli was the unsung hero of this drama. *You*, the congregation, can play a similar role. By being open, instead of closed; by pressing him to go on and tell the whole truth as he understands it, without hiding anything; by refusing to let him evade or stop with a half-statement—you can have a profound effect upon his usefulness to God not only this year but through his entire ministry. Had Eli not been so sensitive to what had happened, and so persistent in pressing for an account, Samuel might well have ended up just a second class duff. And you play the role of Eli today. Every time I share in the ordination of a young minister I wish I had a chance to talk to his congregation about the tremendous responsibility which is theirs in the formation of this person whom God has called as a spokesman. For a man's first church can make him or break him— can force him to go deeper than superficialities, can push him back into real study of the Bible by asking questions; or it can be so content with generalities, and so disinterested in what's important that they wither his spirit in two or three years. I've seen it happen time and time again. Some churches seem to be almost professionals at grinding up young preachers and making them into pulp. David is of course not yet through seminary, but you can still make a profound impact on him. I'm pretty sure Grace Church is not the kind which will kill his spirit with bitter hostility. A greater temptation will be to fail to challenge him where you feel he is in error, rather than strain your friendship or seem to be impolite. I appealed earlier for you not to close your *ears* if you don't like something he has said. I now call on you not to seal your *lips* either—but do your talking not to *others* of like persuasion in little huddles in the corner. Go directly to *David* and say "I think you're wrong; or, I can't

understand all those big words; or, you contradicted yourself in
your reasoning; or, how in the world did you get that idea out of
that passage of Scripture?" You may do a little head-butting. But it
will be good for him—and just *might* be good for you.

Fourth, and last—I want to express my belief that the refreshing word from the Lord which David brings us can be as creative
in its effect as was Samuel's long ago. By his telling his message to
someone who would listen, and demanded to hear all, he grew into
a prophet of the first rank. We can help David grow to his full
stature too. But it's not just a one-way street. As Israel blossomed
in the following years, so I believe this church can. A fresh breath
of air, a new point of view, different insights can stir us all to a fuller
life, a deeper commitment, a closer fellowship. I don't want to put
all the burden of responsibility on David's shoulders, or yours, for
I have my load to carry too. But I am convinced this is a rare spirit
we have in our midst for the next year. Make full use of him.
Demand that he give his best. Then when he does, hear him—and
see if through his lips God does not speak to us.

THE CITY HE WEPT OVER

Date: August 18, 1968—10th Sunday after Trinity

Lectionary: Psalm 90; **II Kings 5:1-14**; **St. Luke 19:37-48**

Hymns: I do not find a copy of the bulletin so do not know what
hymns were used.

*In April of 1968 year Martin Luther King, Jr. had been assassinated,
and in June Robert Kennedy, a candidate for Democratic nomination
as President was. The nation was deeply divided over the Vietnam War
and race. Eight days after this sermon the Democratic National
Convention opened in Chicago, and on the tenth day tens of thousands
of Vietnam War protestors rioted. In addition to the national tension,
Little Rock was shaken when an 18 year old black boy/man was sen-
tenced to the County Farm where he was killed by a trusty. There were
riots in Little Rock, troops were brought in and a curfew enforced.*

"And when he drew near and saw the city he wept over it, saying 'Would that even today you knew the things that make
for peace!'"

You have approached Little Rock from the south, using the
new four-lane Pine Bluff-Sheridan road, haven't you? You'll remember the big hill just this side of Sweet Home—I guess it's
Granite Mountain. Well, every time I come to the crest of that hill,
driving north, I'm struck by the sudden view of Little Rock and
North Little Rock laid out below. Sometimes it's almost breath-

taking. And the wonder is heightened when the traveler's goal is a still larger city—as when an airplane drops out of the clouds to reveal New York City down below; or when the destination is a religious shrine—Iona for a Presbyterian, Rome for a Catholic. Jerusalem was for Jesus all these things. In addition he was receiving the ancient equivalent of a ticker-tape parade down Broadway, the kind of welcome reserved for heroes and honored guests. How would you feel if you rounded a corner and beheld a whole city—your city-turned out to greet you? We would expect Jesus, on this day of entry into Jerusalem, to have similar emotions—a thrill, joy, excitement—wouldn't we?

It's rather startling to hear the Gospel saying instead, "And when he drew near and saw the city he wept over it." But do you remember why? He goes on, "Would that even today you knew the things that make for peace!! But now they are hid from your eyes." The Greek word for "wept" is an unusually strong one. It doesn't mean just getting a lump in your throat, or misty-eyed, or even shedding a few tears. *That* is how Jesus is described at the tomb of Lazarus. *This* word signifies a strong outburst of emotion, or hurt and dismay. We find it in St. Mark's account of Simon Peter after he had denied Jesus for the last time, heard the cock crow and saw Jesus turn to look at him. "And he broke down and wept." It's heart-broken sorrow of that intensity which Jesus is said to have experienced at the moment he came to the point on the road where he could first see Jerusalem. He loved all this city stood for—or at least was intended for. He loved the people, and the activities in which they were engaged. He saw it fitting into God's scheme of things to make the world a better place in which to live. But instead of moving in this direction, instead of heading toward the goal set out for them, he realized they were following a different course which was bound to lead to disaster. "For the days shall come upon you, when your enemies will cast up a bank about you and surround you, and hem you in on every side…" History confirms that within forty years a Roman army under Titus had done just that. He laid siege to Jerusalem at Passover time when there were 3,000,000 Jews in the city; dug a moat or ditch all the way around, and erected a wooden palisade fence. When the defending Jews burned that, he replaced it with a stone wall, and penned them in like cattle ready for slaughter. It was bound to happen—at the hands of one empire or another, sooner or later. God never has tolerated pride or injustice or cruelty or exploitation. He has worked through political events to carry out His judgment, even using as His agents non-believers and men who themselves are wicked. But in one way or another He has always seen to it that an arrogant people are humbled and greedy folk are stripped of that which they have taken. Jesus read the hand-writing on the wall that day he entered Jerusalem, and he cried out in sorrow.

I have experienced many similar feelings this past week about a city I love—our city. It was not that something was occurring which was radically different from what has happened many times before. It's just that it broke open for all to see so clearly. It's troubling to watch armed soldiers riding around in police cars, patrolling our streets. I don't know about you, but I found it very disturbing to be told I had to be in my house by a certain hour. I had never lived under a curfew before. I'm not saying these safety measures were wrong. I'm just observing they were such violent symptoms that surely no one can be under the illusion that there is no illness—any more than a man with 105 degree fever can kid himself he is not sick. And the tragedy of it is that it need not have happened. We know—we have heard about, and seen, and experienced "the things that make for peace." We have had what Jesus called "a time of visitation," an opportunity to believe and obey. But so many of us have chosen to ignore the word spoken to us; or to dilute it; or just to apply it to the other person. I have spent a great many hours this week thinking about, discussing, our city. I have wanted to weep over it—and not just it, but our whole national life. All the warning signals are flashing, yet we seem to pay them little heed.

But perhaps you are protesting, inside yourself, at this moment, "Well, I'm not ignoring them. I am deeply alarmed. I just don't know what I can do." I'm certainly acquainted with that frustration. The

118

problems of race and poverty, of industrialization and ghettos, seem so vast and complex they demand governmental action, or remedial measures requiring billions of dollars. And certainly some of them do. I would be the last to say we can leave all our laws and social structures just the way they've been for the last 50 years—or worse yet, to try to set the clock back. You know me better than that, I trust. But right at the point when I was about to throw up my hands in futility, I found great help and comfort in reading again the story of Naaman the Syrian general, who was healed of leprosy by Elisha the prophet. We read it for our first lesson this morning. You'll remember how furious Naaman grew when Elisha's prescription was nothing more complex than "Go and wash in the Jordan seven times." And then his servants rebuked him by asking, "My father, if the prophet had commanded you to do some great thing, would you not have done it? How much rather, then, when he says to you, 'Wash, and be clean.'" There are lots of things I, as one of the Presbyterian ministers of this city, that we as a small congregation, cannot do. We can't pass laws, or provide funds of any size. But instead of giving up in disgust, or exploding in impatience, can we not set ourselves to doing some of the "things that make for peace" which *are* in our ability? What if they are just "little *things*" and we are just "little *people*"?

Albert Schweitzer wrote, "Always keep your eyes open for the little task, because it is the little task that is important to Jesus Christ. The future of the Kingdom of God does not depend on the enthusiasm of this or that powerful person. These great ones are necessary too, but it is equally necessary to have a great number of little people who will do a little thing in the service of Christ…The great flowing rivers represent only a small part of all the water that is necessary to nourish and sustain the earth. Beside the flowing river there is the water *in* the earth, the subterranean water, and there are the little streams which continually enter the river and feed it and prevent it from sinking into the earth. Without these others waters, the silent, hidden subterranean waters and the trickling streams, the great river could no longer flow. Thus it is with the little tasks to be fulfilled by all of us." ("The Treasure Chest" pg. 187)

And what are some of the "little tasks" within your grasp and mine which don't just salve our consciences the way Christmas baskets do, but make a real if limited contribution? Let me make five specific suggestions.

First, learn to call people you deal with by the terms they choose and like. I happen to like to be called "Don." I've known a few people in my life who have insisted on calling me "Donnie" and a few others who say "Preacher Don." I don't like either one, and I soon begin to resent the people who address me that way because it shows they have no respect for my preferences, and hence for me. It's the same when we are dealing with groups of people. Japanese don't like to be called "Japs," nor Italians "Wops. We all know people of African descent resent the term "nigger." Many middle class whites don't realize they are almost as offended by the way we pronounce N-e-g-r-o as "nigra." I was in a meeting this week with an official of our city who waxed eloquent about the course given his subordinates by a psychiatrist who taught them to avoid the "trigger terms" which insult people. But in his presentation he must have said "nigra" a dozen times. When a black man pointed out this was in itself such a "trigger term" for his community the white man never caught the point. His ears just couldn't pick up the distinction between "Negro" and "nigra." If you can't either, then perhaps you'd better learn to say "black people" for that seems to be the label in fashion right now. Just remember, a person has a right to pick the name by which he is known. When I ask you to quit calling me "Donnie" but you insist on doing it, you are creating friction which need not exist. I may be able to forgive you—but you have no right to cause the offense which I must overcome. This business of calling people what they want to be called, and pronouncing it the way they like it, is very small. But it's something every one of you can do. It is one of the "little things which make for peace."

Second, learn to listen to people who disagree with you, who are on the opposite side of an issue, who belong to the other camp. This doesn't mean you have to agree with them—though more

120

often than you would expect you may find you really do. The fact you are respectfully attentive while a man presents his case does not commit you to accepting as accurate his description of the problem. You are not betraying anybody, or any loyalty, when you give an opponent a hearing. What you are doing again is showing that you regard him as a full person, worthy of respect. You may later disagree with everything he says, and tear his argument to shreds. But you give him a place on the agenda and don't try to crowd him off. Now this is time consuming, and it's exhausting. But if there's anything I've learned through pastoral counseling it's that the most creative thing I do when my study door is closed is listen. Very seldom are people helped by words of wisdom from my lips. A fair number do seem to regain some self-respect and hope and strength by my willingness to listen, an attitude I can have because God has listened to me. I don't necessarily approve of the adultery committed, or the theft carried out by my visitor. But my readiness to listen says, "Though I may abhor what you have done, I value you as a person." This week as I have sat in bi-racial groups, I have been struck by how difficult people in our city from different walks of life find it to listen to each other. If both blacks and whites could develop the art of hearing one another there might be a real break-through in race relations. I wish you would let me arrange a one-to-one visit between you and someone from B.U.Y. This is another one of the "things that make for peace" within the grasp of every child, every student, every adult. It's very demanding, but it is rewarding.

Third, learn the facts. You'll pick up a great many if you simply become skilled in listening, though some require exhaustive research and even detective work. Again, this week I have been struck by how much misinformation, and partial information, goes into the decisions we all make. Many of us think because we live in a community we automatically know what's happening in it. We assume because we drive by a certain school, or through a neighborhood, we are experts on its problem. But of course such assumptions are false. Often the accuracy of a statement can be checked with one phone call, or one visit to a problem area—although some demand a lot more than that. You may not be able to get to the bottom of some mysteries. But where you can, see that you do— and you'll find that you are sharing in another of "the things that make for peace."

Fourth, do not sit by silently, passively, in the presence of gross wrongs and injustices. You may not have the authority or influence to get them changed, but you can sure yell to high heaven. You may attract so much attention that improvements will be started. At the least you'll let the victim know he's not forgotten; somebody cares. The event which triggered the violence in our community this past week was the murder of an eighteen old Negro boy name Curtis Ingram, Jr. at the County Farm. Nobody claims he was justified in driving without a license or possessing drugs. But he was given a sentence which no eighteen year old in *this* church would have re-ceived for the same offenses. And that is not right. He was sent to a prison farm which we have all known for years was a disgrace, which a Grand Jury has said was filthy beyond belief. It's not many miles from this church. Our janitors had sons there his past year who were frightened for their lives. Yet we have sat here and per-mitted this condition to go on. In *scale* it's far different, but the *prin-ciple* is the same as the silent toleration by German Christians of the Nazi concentration camps in their midst. The responsibility rests not primarily on a trusty, nor on a county judge, but on us— the good people who remained silent about a festering sore we knew existed but preferred to forget. So long as there is freedom of speech, every one in this room has the power of protest which he can use.

Fifth, not all of you—but a great many—are in positions to open jobs to people who have been excluded from them. You may have to help train them, but a Christian is always ready to go the second mile. This is the real core of the racial friction in our com-munity. It's the key to housing, to political influence, to schools. It's true that man does not live by bread alone—but he has an aw-fully hard time living without any, or just some crumbs. Jesus said feeding the hungry was doing an act of service to him. Well, far better than giving a man a hand-out is to give him a decent job, a job with a future, a job with equal pay so he can buy his own bread. And many of you could open some first-rate jobs to people who have been forced to settle for second-rate ones, or create some kind of job for those with none. When you look at the vast complexities of the racial crisis of our nation, it may seem very little for you to enable one Negro girl to quit being a maid and become a secretary instead; one man with a college degree to exchange his overalls for a business suit and the job that goes with it. But I can tell you this is an act which makes for peace because it is an act of concern and respect and Christian love.

"And when he drew near and saw the city he wept over it, saying 'Would that even today you knew the things that make for peace.'" The weeping of Jesus is the weeping of God. I have been conscious this week that he who cried out in sorrow for Jerusalem was also looking down on our city, grieving because we worry so much about solutions we do not yet have that we are failing to grasp hold of the things that make for peace which we can understand. Never scorn the little things, for God often chooses them as instruments of His healing grace. "Even today" you and I can begin to take steps toward fulfilling God's will on earth that will make a real impact on the life of our community and perhaps avert the disaster toward which we seem headed.

God of Shadrach, Meshach, and Abednego

Date: November 30, 1969—First Sunday in Advent

Lectionary: Psalm 2; **Daniel 2:48-3:1,8-13,16-28; Acts 5:17-42**

Hymns: I do not have the bulletin for that Sunday so do not
know what hymns were sung.

On March 16, 1968 a private—we'll call him Joe—in Company
C, First Battalion, 20th Infantry of the United States Army
was moving through the countryside of South Vietnam in the
darkness which precedes the dawn. As the first light of morning
came he could see ahead the little Village of Song My. Joe had
never liked killing. It went contrary to all he had been taught as
a child. It violated his respect for human life. But on the other
hand, he also respected his country. He had been called into military service and he had responded. It had not been easy the first
time he saw a man fall to the ground after he had pulled the trigger of his rifle. It had not been easy to watch our B-52 planes drop
bombs from way up in the sky on villages where the Viet Cong
were hiding, with the sure knowledge that some of the victims
who would be blown to bits or crippled for life would be little children. But Joe had gone along with these distasteful experiences
because as General Sherman said a century ago, "war is hell" and

when one goes into it he must realize that injustices and cruelty are bound to be carried out.

In the darkness of March 16 Joe was heavy of heart about the assignment ahead of them. These "search and destroy" missions were always messy. But when a war is being fought, and the enemy has been killing your buddies by snipers hidden in a village, there's not much alternative to going in and wiping them out unless you are going to sit there and let them pick you off one by one. Joe gritted his teeth and prepared to carry out orders.

Then light began to break—not only physically, as the sun approached the horizon, but also in terms of the truth about the situation. The orders from Joe's non-commissioned and commissioned officers were to kill every occupant of the village ahead. Joe could now see that this was not just a military outpost of the Viet Cong, but a community peopled mostly by old men, women and children. He was part of the squad told to clear all people out of the houses and gather them into three groups. Then came the order to shoot. Joe could not believe what he heard. He wanted to vomit. He wanted to run. He wanted to cry as little children pled not to be shot—and were.

There were three possible courses of action Joe could take. One was to sigh a sigh too keep for words, to breathe a prayer of apology to the Heavenly Father whose children stood before him, and then pull the trigger as he was ordered by his commanding officers. He had been trained to obey without questioning. Instructors had explained that in battle there is no time for discussion, and often not only one's own safety but the lives of others depend upon instant fulfillment of an assignment. On the other hand, he vaguely remembered from class that the Uniform Code of Military Justice contained the qualifying adjective "lawful" about orders which must be obeyed. He also vaguely remembered that at the Nuremberg Trials in Germany after World War II the American government had taken the position that moral responsibility for an act could not be shrugged off by pleading "but I was ordered to do it by my superiors." So Joe realized a second course of action he could take was simply to refuse to participate in what seemed to him to be a massacre on the grounds that this was contrary to what he believed Almighty God wanted him to do. But refusal to obey an order is a serious matter in the military, especially in wartime, and more especially when engaged in a military action—as this presumably was considered to be. He could be court-martialed. He could be shot on the spot, for anyone who would order the death of women and children would not be overly concerned with the fate of one disobedient buck private. Then Joe noticed something going on behind a tree nearby. Here was a third possible route. One of his buddies had just shot himself in the foot. He would report it as an accident, maybe. He might say a shot came out of the nearby wood—a Viet Cong sniper. As a wounded man, no one would require him to do the dirty work which had been assigned. Joe could do the same—disqualify himself by playing sick, or getting wounded.

These various possibilities ran through Joe's mind that early morning of March 16 in less time than it has taken me to outline them. He had to make a decision—quickly—for the sergeant and lieutenant were not patient men. What would *you* have counseled Joe to do? If he had cried out "I want my Church to help guide me in this most difficult decision I've ever faced?"—what would the Church have to say? Is there anything in the Bible, anything we've had revealed about by God, which might have been of assistance to Joe in those few seconds when his whole future was hanging in the balance? If the Christian religion has nothing to say at a moment like that what good is it?

I am speaking to you today not in judgment but in agony. I hope it is coming through in my words and in my tone of voice. I do not feel self-righteous, as though I had all the answers and the men in Company C were benighted, and their officers vicious. I hurt for the people on whom the spot-light of public attention has been focused, and for their families. I hurt also for the few survivors of the village of Song My; and for the man who shot himself in the foot and who has been wondering ever since if he was a coward;

126

and for the enlisted men, like Joe, whose names have not yet come to light. I hurt for the thousands of other times when similar tragedies have occurred but never been reported—in this war, the Korean War, and World War II, and the Civil War. While the emphasis just now is on the possible guilt of some American troops, I remember the atrocities which have been committed by the Viet Cong during the Tet Offensive; and the North Koreans; and the Germans and Japanese; and by the Yankees and Confederates a century ago. This is a far bigger issue than what one lieutenant and one sergeant told their men to do on March 16, 1968. "War is cruel and you cannot refine it" General Sherman replied to the city government of Atlanta in 1864. Fifteen years later, after time for reflection, in an address to the Michigan Military Academy he made his classic statement, "I am tired and sick of war. It's glory is all moonshine. It is only those who have neither fired a shot nor heard the shrieks and groans of the wounded who cry aloud for blood, more vengeance, more desolation. War is hell." On the other hand, surrendering a civilian population—a whole nation—to enemy forces who are bent upon their destruction is also hell. There are no simple answers which I have found. My lack of self-righteousness is no virtue of mine. I probably would be, if I were sure what was right. I tend to be in other areas where it is more a matter of black-and-white, instead of shades of gray. I have said very little about Vietnam because I've never felt "the word of the Lord is upon me" with a clear message to convey. I just hurt—for my country, for my fellow citizens in military service, for the people of Vietnam, for the people of the whole world. And I ask myself, "Is there no word from the Lord which could be of help to Joe, and other like him?"

The Presbyterian Church, in the Westminster Confession of Faith, has said, "It is the duty of the people to pray for magistrates... to obey their lawful commands, and to be subject to their authority, for conscience sake." This goes back to New Testament teachings that the Christian has an obligation to those over him—in government, in families, and even to slave owners. Paul looked upon institutions—in state, economics, and home—as gifts from

God by which we protect ourselves from chaos. Even if the individuals who give us orders are evil, we have a duty to obey—unless the order itself is "unlawful." That's the word which appears again in the American Uniform Code of Military Justice—"lawful," "unlawful." Obedience to authority is required *up to a point*. Beyond that when orders from men blatantly contradict the will of God, a man must choose where his ultimate loyalty lies. And for the man of faith, final allegiance must always be to God and to His will. This is what the General Assembly tried to say again a couple of years ago in its pronouncement on "civil disobedience," but such a furor arose as a result that many people have never calmed down long enough to read or to hear the message. If there never comes a time when a servant of God reaches the point of having to declare "This I will not do, whatever the consequences for me may be"—then Joe need not have wrestled with his conscience at Song My village; and we had no business at Nuremberg trying the people who ran the concentration camps of Germany. If we must always obey orders, whatever they are, under every circumstance, then we have ceased to be moral agents, and have become robots and machines.

The Bible never regards men of faith as being reduced to that. It honors and holds up as examples those who are close enough to the Lord God Almighty to know His will for them, and who love Him enough to carry it out, even if it means great hardship. We read this morning from the Book of Daniel the story of Shadrach, Meshach and Abednego—young Jews taken into exile by the Babylonians and trained to be civil servants. Through Daniel, who had won the king's favor, these three were eventually put in charge of all the affairs of the province of Babylon. Then came an order that they were to bow down to, and worship, a golden image which King Nebuchadnezzar had had made of himself. This the three young men refused to do—even when they knew their punishment was to be thrown into the fiery furnace. The story goes on to say that they miraculously survived this treatment. And Nebuchadnezzar was so overwhelmed by their trust in, and deliverance by, Yahweh that he said, "Blessed be the God of Shadrach, Meshach, and Abednego, who has sent his angel and delivered his servants, who trusted in him, and set at naught the king's command, and yielded up their bodies rather than serve and worship any god except their own God."

And then from the New Testament, we read a similar story from the Acts of the Apostles. These followers of Jesus were ordered by the duly constituted authorities—the high priest, the council and the senate—to cease preaching in the Temple. They were thrown in prison one night, pending a trial—but a messenger of the Lord let them out, and the next morning they were back at it. The police went out after them, and brought them before the Sanhedrin where charges of civil disobedience were brought against them, and orders given once more that they "cease and desist." Then the New Testament says, "But Peter and the apostles answered, 'We must obey God rather than men.'" They didn't try to hide it. They came very close to getting executed on the spot, and would have had it not been for a rabbi named Gamaliel who argued "Don't rush. Time will show whether this movement is of men or of God." So instead, they just took a beating—the Greek says, literally, they had the hide taken off them. And the text adds, "Then they left the presence of the council, rejoicing that they were counted worthy to suffer dishonor for the name. And every day in the temple and at home they did not cease teaching and preaching Jesus as the Christ." That is as clear a case of civil disobedience as you can find in any document. The legal authorities had gone beyond the boundaries of the "lawful" in what they ordered. Loyalty to a higher law, to the law of God, took over.

Now, back to Joe, the private in Vietnam, on the outskirts of Song My, faced by a moral dilemma that was tearing him apart on the morning of March 16. And forward, to all the sons and daughters who will be forced to make similar choices in the future—children, like the little boy who is to be baptized today. What do we have to say about God, and our ties with Him, which can be of help to guide those we love—and to guide ourselves—in the terribly complex issues of our time? Four things I believe I can affirm.

First, I agree that government and institution are God's normal way of bringing order out of chaos as men live together. Therefore we have an obligation to obey orders given by duly constituted authority. If I don't like them, I should try from within to change them. I should always start from the assumption that the institution which has helped me is, if not totally right, at least within the permissible range. The burden of proof is on me if I say that it has gone astray. Second, however, the Lord God Almighty, the God and Father of our Lord Jesus Christ, is my Creator and Savior and Sustainer. To Him I own my very being, and my ultimate loyalty. If there ever has to be a choice between God and any institution— even Church or country—then my ultimate allegiance must be to Him and His will. There can be no question as to this for a Christian. Third, if service to God brings me into conflict with the laws of men, I hope I am ready to bear the consequences and pay the price. For Shadrach, Meshach and Abednego, it meant being thrown into the fiery furnace. For the apostles, it meant jail and a beating. Joe, in Vietnam that morning, had no right to place loyalty to God before obedience of his commanding officers unless he was prepared to take the punishment he knew might follow. God does not call us to be cowards; to whine and sniffle. When we take up the cross of Jesus Christ, we should all know that may entail a crucifixion. Let it come as no surprise to me if I suffer. But on the other hand, I never have the right to decide when the time has come for *you* to make that sacrifice. I would not presume to tell Joe what he should have done at Song My. I can hurt for him, cry with him, but not choose for him. But he must decide. Fourth, I can affirm my faith that God can and will use the courageous witness of His people for the building of His kingdom. He can do this, even though some of the martyrs—past and present—have probably made unwise choices; and some of them have had mixed motives. Some who have risked their "lives, their fortunes, and their sacred honor," to paraphrase our Declaration of Independence, God has brought through alive and respected. This He did for Shadrach, Meshach, and Abednego. Some have suffered, but survived—as

130

Peter and the apostles did. Some died an ignominious death—and many are forgotten. But "the seed of the Church is the blood of the martyrs." No faithful obedience is wasted by God, though men may overlook it. Someday, somehow, God will bring peace to this earth, and he will enable men to live as brothers. If I offer my life to that end, whether I am led to do that through obedience to lawful commands or in witness against what I can only read as unlawful ones, I believe God will take my sacrifice and use it.

These four things I want to say to my children, because I believe God has revealed them to us. Perhaps they are part of the moral and spiritual equipment you will want to offer to your sons and daughters, and to all the Joes of this earth, as they prepare to live in a world which forces us to make profound choices on a moment's notice. "Blessed be the God of Shadrach, Meshach and Abednego." May we be so closely tied to our Father, and so loyal to His ways, that if anyone ever says "Blessed be the God of Don and Susie and Bill" it will mean the same thing.

Jesus Was a Jew

Date: November 29, 1970—First Sunday in Advent

Lectionary: **Zechariah 10:6-12; Matthew 21:1-13**

Hymns: I do not have the bulletin for that Sunday so do not
know what hymns were sung.

For the last couple of weeks our eleventh and twelfth grade
morning Church School class has been discussing the question
of what Jesus looked like. Someone questioned whether He really
did resemble Sallman's "Head of Christ"—you now the one with
the tan robe and the beard and long hair down to His shoulders,
so that He makes one think of some of the more "way out" younger
generation. The answer, of course, is that no one knows how Jesus
appeared. There are no pictures, nor even any word descriptions,
left behind. What artists have always done is to depict Him in
terms of their own culture. That's why most of the pictures we've
seen show an Anglo-Saxon, clean-cut, All-American Boy type.
But I referred our young people to a book we have in the church
library entitled *Each with His Own Brush*, in which Dan Fleming,
a missionary scholar, has pulled together art from the Christian
communities in China, Japan, Korea, India and Africa. There we
find in one painting the Holy Family gathered in a pagoda, and the
Christ Child has almond shaped eyes while Joseph, looking on,
wears a pigtail. Or a crucifix from Africa below the Sahara will re-

veal the victim nailed to the cross as being a man with kinky hair and thick, Negroid lips. I'll never forget what a shock it was to me when, as a child, I first heard of a black Madonna. It struck me then as scandalous—almost blasphemous. Now, of course, I realize it was a healthy, glorious way in which some black artist was proclaiming, "Jesus came to be like me!" It was the same affirmation which led Leonardo da Vinci to present Him as a sixteenth century Italian. Jesus Christ, the Son of God, is universal.

But that is just *part* of the truth. For Jesus was also a Jew, a resident of first century Galilee. He, therefore, must have looked like all the other Jews of that time and region. We don't know exactly what their appearance was, except that probably they were of dark complexion and perhaps had the Semitic facial structure of today's residents of Iraq and Jordan and Egypt. But there is no question that He was a Jew of the Jews. "Hosanna to the Son of David!" sang the crowds as He entered into Jerusalem on Palm Sunday. Traditionally, this story of the triumphal entry at the beginning of His last week has been the Gospel reading on the first Sunday of Advent, and it is a great way to begin our preparation for Christmas. For whereas God could certainly have come among men as a Chinese or an Indian or a black African, or even a blonde resident of Northern Europe, the testimony of the Gospels is that in fact He came as a Jew. "Son of David," of course, referred back to the greatest king Israel ever had. The entry with Jesus riding on the donkey was to fulfill a prophecy contained in the final chapters attached to the Book of Zechariah. This section was probably written a little before 300 years earlier, when nationalism was on the increase among the Jews. We read for our first lesson this morning from a later chapter of the same book: "I will strengthen the house of Judah, and I will save the house of Joseph." (Zechariah 10:6) Jesus was not content with just this restricted view of the purpose of God—but He never denied His identity with His religious and national heritage. He sent His disciples "first to the house of Israel." He said He came not to destroy the Law, but to fulfill it. If you have any doubt as to His Jewishness, read the first seventeen verses of the first chapter of St. Matthew's Gospel where you find the "begats," tracing Jesus' family tree (interestingly enough, through Joseph, not Mary) back for 42 generations to Abraham.

What did Jesus look like? I don't know—except His appearance was whatever Jews looked like in those days. For "Jesus was a Jew." The Bible leaves us in no doubt on this point.

But the Christian Church, down through the centuries, has often had a struggle swallowing this fact and living with it. At first, of course it wasn't hard for all the original members of the Church were themselves Jews. The earliest disciples had no intention of separating from Jewish life and worship, but sought to be a reform movement from within to bring renewal to the covenant community. The Apostle Paul always went first to the synagogue when he came to a new city to bring the Good News about Jesus, and usually there were some who believed. But gradually two rather distinct fellowships emerged. For over two hundred years, the Jews were in a more favored position in the Roman Empire than were the Christians, because while Jews were only tolerated at least they were that—whereas Christianity was outlawed.

A radical change took place in 313 A.D. when the Roman Emperor, Constantine, was converted and he proclaimed that the whole empire would instantly do likewise. For the first time, the Christian Church was in a position to lord it over other religions— and did, including Judaism. The Christian people inherited some long-standing anti-Semitic feeling from the Romans, whose great intellectuals such as Cicero and Seneca had indulged in a little Jew-baiting along the way. Add to this the memory that most of the ecclesiastical leaders of Judaism had rejected Jesus, and the even more recent memory of treatment some of the Christians had experienced during the "underground" period, and we can understand—without approving—the retaliation indulged in right after Christianity was made the official faith of the Roman empire. Laws were passed to segregate Jews. They were to be protected from total extinction, in the belief that some had to be around when the Lord came back in all His glory—but they were stripped of citizenship and made permanent aliens. Down through the Dark Ages and medieval period the Church gave in to these very human, selfish drives. Ghettos were created in which Jews were forced to live. Often they had to wear a yellow mark, usually the Star of David, for easy identification. They were barred from citizenship, and many forms of work.

Theologically, the Church did better. Around the year 150 a man named Marcion tried to pare away all Jewish aspects from Christianity. He wanted to discard the Old Testament, entirely. He rejected certain Christian writings *in toto*, such as the Epistle to the Hebrews. He then went through others and pulled out all favorable references to Jews and Judaism. But the main stream of the Church said "No!" It was because of his attempt that the first efforts were made to draw up a canon, or list of approved books, which finally resulted in our collection of 27 books in the New Testament, plus 39 in the Old.

But the *practice* fell short of the theology. In the late middle ages country after country in Western Europe expelled Jews entirely from their borders. Ferdinand and Isabella, the rulers of Spain who commissioned Columbus to sail west, in 1492, the same year he discovered the New World, drove every Jew who refused to be converted out of their kingdom—and all for the glory of Christ. It has been convenient for us in the Christian community to forget, or fail to learn, about these facts of history. But if we want to understand the resentment some of our Jewish friends feel toward Christian evangelism, we must face up to the rather harsh methods resorted to in the past. Indeed, the lot of Jews in so-called Christendom did not really improve much until the late 1700s, when the American and French Revolutions elevated the dignity of each man. But even then it was not all smooth sailing. For the in the 1800s new so-called scientific theories were advocated regarding Jews as a dangerous people, and an inferior race. They took hold especially in Germany and Poland where sizeable Jewish communities existed—but where the Christian Church, which should have known better, was also very strong. Such ideas spread into Holy Russia where on Easter Eve, 1881, a massacre of Jews was triggered by a tavern brawl and 167 Jewish towns were left in smoldering ruins. In 1908 a document, which later turned out to be forged by the Russian secret police, was published under the title "Protocols of the Learned Elders of Zion." Some of you older members of this congregation may remember hearing of it. It was widely read in the Christian world, and many took seriously its references to a revolutionary plot. Between 1900 and 1933 there was a smoldering fire which really broke into flame when Adolph Hitler came to power in Germany. In 1935 in Germany, the birthplace of the Protestant Reformation, citizenship was taken away from all Jews. In 1938 burnings and lootings of their property were permitted without interference on the part of police. As World War II got underway, anti-Semitism grew worse and worse. In one city in Poland there were 160,000 Jews on June 29, 1941 when the Nazis took over. Three years later when the Russians liberated it, there were 827 left. Try to imagine more people than there are in Little Rock reduced to 827 in 3 years. By 1945, it is estimated that 6 out of every 7 Jews in Europe had been killed.

Now during this period not all Christians sat by silently, condoning if not approving. Six hundred priests in Greece went to prison rather than read a sermon which was anti-Jewish. Roman Catholics and Protestants in the Netherlands risked their own lives to hide Jewish neighbors from the Gestapo. King Christian of Denmark so identified with the Jewish citizens of his kingdom that he wore a yellow Star of David on his own clothes, and refused to permit laws which would have sent them to prison. But the Christian community on the whole was slow to awake to the terrible sin committed against the Jewish people—and far too often, there seemed to be little effort made to stop it.

And Anti-Semitism did not come to an end with the death of Hitler in 1945. It has grown more intense in Soviet Russia since 1948—and also in much of Eastern Europe and the Middle East. The existence of Israel as a state has made feelings more heated, but it has only fanned flames which were already there. Nor can we only point to the other side of the Iron Certain. Some of the purveyors of anti-Jewish propaganda in earlier decades are still around. They may be a bit more discreet about this article of their creed than previously, but they have never repudiated it, and from time to time it pops up to the surface again. I refer to the Ku Klux Klan, which was so viciously anti-Semitic in the 1920s, and to Gerald L. K. Smith who had his hey-day in the 1930s. If you want to know why the Jewish community of our city has been so upset about the Christ of the Ozarks statue near Eureka Springs, and the paving of a road up to it, it's because they remember all too well how this same man, Smith, gave approval to what Hitler did to Jews in Europe—approval in the name of Jesus Christ! And then it gets closer to home still when we examine the admission policies of the country clubs here in Little Rock; and that of the Junior League, unless it has changed quite recently. Now exclusion from these bastions of society is certainly not on the level with denial of citizenship, seizing of property, and sentencing to a concentration camp. But a closed door is a symbol that deep within the hearts and minds of many who profess to be followers of this man named Jesus, there is a feeling that Jews are somehow inferior. And now, within recent weeks, in our own city we have had the Orthodox Jewish Synagogue at the corner of Eight and Louisiana Streets, broken into. A treasured scroll of Old Testament scriptures has been stolen. Swastikas, the emblem of Nazi Germany, were carved on the woodwork. This was an inexcusable action on the part of the vandals who did it. But far more dangerous, in my opinion, has been the apathy of the community—including the Christian community—since it was discovered. This may be a one-shot performance on the part of a handful of sick people. But then it could be the first symptom of a malignancy spreading through the body. And I have heard no widespread alarm. I propose to you that it is the obligation of Christian people to be alert and ready to swing into action to bring this insidious illness to a halt if it spreads in the least. And in the meantime, it would be a gracious thing for us, as followers of Jesus the Jew, to express our sympathy and concern to the Jewish community as we would if any other tragedy struck.

137

Now how are we as Christians going to deal with anti-Semitism when we encounter it? First, I would say don't try to pretend there are no differences between their beliefs and ours—for there are. But it is not necessary to have perfect agreement in order to have respect, and mutual concern. Fortunately, God is Judge, and we can leave it to Him to decide. We can witness to what we believe without demolishing what someone else cherishes. Second, we can make ourselves better informed as to the facts—of what Jews really do believe, and how they worship and live, and not swallow all the old wives' tales which have been passed down for generations. We can become acquainted with Jewish history since Bible times, and learn some of the bitter experiences they have received at the hands of Christians. Third, we can re-read the Bible, including the New Testament, and realize the absolute absurdity of combining Christianity with Anti-Semitism. How can the followers of a man named Jesus be even politely, even silently, anti-Jewish? It is as self-contradictory as it would be to name a pacifist as commanding general of an army. Fourth, we can extend a hand of friendship to members of the Jewish community who feel they are passing through a pretty rough time just now. Maybe you don't know what to say. But then, you often don't know what to say when death strikes in the home of a friend. Yet you go and by your presence you announce "I care." And it means something. It means more than many of us ever realize. The same might hold true when it is not just one family but a whole religious community, which has been shaken to its core.

This is the first Sunday in Advent, the season when we all make preparations to celebrate the birth of Jesus Christ, the Son of God. Hopefully, it is a season when we shall also prepare to make room for Him in our own lives. Remember this, in the days to come. When Jesus rode into Jerusalem on the back of a donkey, the crowds shouted "Hosanna to the Son of David!" The little babe born in Bethlehem was a Jew-boy. There is no way to make room for the Christ which does not clear away prejudices and fears and scorn of Jews, not just two thousand years ago, but also today.

The Audacity of God's Men

Date: January 31, 1971—Fourth Sunday after Epiphany

Lectionary: Psalm 46; **Genesis 18:22-33**; **St. Mark 4:35-41**

Hymns: I do not have the bulletin for that Sunday so do not
know what hymns were sung.

*Two notebooks containing my 1971 sermons from April through
December were destroyed in my 1998 fire so the range from which I
could select an example for 1971 was limited.*

Last Monday morning I awoke to find myself sick with a full
blown sinus infection. Those of you who share this misery can
appreciate how wretched I felt. Most of the day I spent in bed, not
really doing much except dozing. Finally, in the evening I did make
myself get out the lectionary to begin studying for today's sermon.
The first passage suggested was the story from Genesis in which
Abraham bargains with God for deliverance of the city of Sodom.
You'll remember it from our first Scripture lesson this morning. The
sins of Sodom are notorious, and it is obvious that the judgment
of God is about to wipe it out, when Abraham intervenes. He says
to God, "If there are fifty righteous people there, are you still going
to do it?…Far be it from you to do such a thing, to slay the righteous with the wicked…Shame on you!" So God backs off and says,
"Alright, if there are fifty, I won't." Then Abraham pushes a little
harder. "What if there are forty-five?" And God gives in again. By

this time Abraham has tasted success. He keeps pushing harder and harder, until he finally got God to agree that if there are as few as ten in the city, He will not destroy Sodom.

Well, I read and re-read this story, as best I could through watery eyes. And then I sat up in bed, and through my stopped-up nose I announced to an empty room, "They've got to be kidding!" Of course I had read the story before, but I couldn't imagine what joker or committee would have slipped it into the lectionary with the idea of making some poor pastor try to preach on it. So in desperation I moved on to other passages for the day, and I came to the one in St. Mark's Gospel in which Jesus, asleep in the boat on the Sea of Galilee, is awakened by His disciples who are terrified by a storm which has caught them. He rebukes the wind and demands, "Peace! Be still." When there was suddenly a great calm, the disciples asked "Who then is this, that even wind and sea obey him?"

All at once I saw a connection which I don't think ever came to me before—one summarized in the title of my sermon today, "The Audacity of God's Men." Now I realize "audacity" is not a word most of us use every day in our conversation. We're vaguely acquainted with it, but might have trouble defining it precisely. The dictionary says it means boldness or daring, especially with confidant or arrogant disregard for personal safety, conventional thought or other restrictions. It borders on effrontery or insolence. Synonyms are temerity or foolhardiness. An antonym, or opposite, is cowardice.

The stories of Abraham and Jesus started me to thinking back across the Bible, and I was struck with how many of God's men were audacious. Just think about this conversation between God and Abraham, to begin with. Can you imagine yourself saying to the Lord God Almighty, Creator of heaven and earth, "Let's see if we can't work out some kind of deal. I'll make a bargain with you. If I can find fifty good men, you call off the fire and brimstone. OK?" Then, as if horse-trading with the Divine wasn't enough, Abraham proceeded to try to shame God into agreeing. And every time God would concede, Abraham would push Him one step further. If that isn't gall, bordering on insolence, I don't know what is.

140

Then I thought of Moses, and his effrontery in marching into the presence of Pharaoh to demand "Let my people go!" Folks in our day get real upset when others come up demanding rights and privileges and property which they think belong to them. Watch what happens to the blood pressure of a manufacturer when a union demands a larger share of his profits. Notice how attached a farmer can get to a piece of pasture when the highway department tries to buy it for right-of-way, and then sues for it in court. Well, these Hebrew slaves were Pharaoh's property. And here was someone not only trying to steal them away in the name of a God whom Pharaoh did not know—but the messenger was a former adopted son of the court who had been chased out of the country for committing murder. Can you imagine the nerve it would take for Moses to stalk into Pharaoh's throne room and demand, "Let my people go"?

And then my mind turned to Elijah, the grizzly Old Testament prophet who fought so with Queen Jezebel and the false worship she brought in. You'll remember the scene on Mount Carmel when he called for a show-down between God and Baal. There were four hundred fifty prophets of Baal. He told them to cut up a bull in one place, and he alone would in another, and they would see which God would send down fire to consume the offering. All morning the four hundred fifty chanted and prayed and cut themselves asking Baal to send fire—and Elijah teased and tormented them because nothing happened. Then he took his turn. First he had water poured over all the wood three times until it was standing in the trench, to prove there were no tricks. And then he prayed, "O Lord, God of Abraham, Isaac, and Israel, let it be known this day that thou art God in Israel, and that I am thy servant, and that I have done all these things at thy word. *Answer me, O Lord, answer me,* that this people may know..." The story goes on to say that the fire then fell and consumed the burnt offering. But the thing I want you to notice is the *nerve*, the *daring*, of Elijah to put God to the test before a whole nation.

And this isn't something we can easily dismiss as "just Old Testament theatrics." We've already seen Jesus at work in the boat

141

with His disciples when they were caught in a storm on the Sea of Galilee. He didn't meekly beg, "Father, can you slow the wind down a little bit, and let the waves slack off just a tad so that if everybody rows hard enough we can make it back to shore?" He didn't put a lot of qualifications and conditions on His request, with plenty of loopholes and escape clauses in case God didn't come through. With firm conviction in His voice, apparently, He *demanded* "Peace, be still!" The writer of the Gospel notes the men in the boat were "filled with awe, and said to one another, 'Who then is this, that even wind and sea obey him?'"

And it is not just because Jesus was the Son of God that He acted in this manner. The Spirit He left with His disciples made them act in the same audacious manner. You'll remember shortly after Pentecost Peter and John were going into the Temple one day to pray when a beggar asked them for money. "But Peter said, 'I have no silver and gold, but I give you what I have; in the name of Jesus Christ of Nazareth, walk.' And he took him by the right hand and raised him up; and immediately his feet and ankles were made strong. And leaping up he stood and walked and entered the temple with them, walking and leaping and praising God." Now try to put yourself in Peter's shoes—or sandals. What kind of nerve did it take for him to say, "In the name of Jesus Christ of Nazareth, walk"? Peter had never healed anyone before. What if it didn't work? What would happen to the new-born church? What ridicule would be heaped on Jesus! It certainly took "confident disregard for personal safety and conventional thought" to deal with God in these terms and put Him on the spot.

Nor did all this end as New Testament days drew to a close. Just as cattle out on the range can be known as belonging to a particular ranch by their brand, so God's men through the two thousand years of the Church's history can be spotted by their audacity in His behalf. Let me cite just three.

Francis of Assisi is perhaps the best loved of all saints by the Protestant world. Most of you know something of his story—how he grew up the spoiled son of a rich merchant in an Italian city around 1200 A.D. When he turned his life over to God he went all the way, giving up every single possession and trusting totally in God to sustain him. Some of you may not know that in the year 1219 he went on the Fifth Crusade (which was attempting to take the Holy Land from the Muslims) for the express purpose of trying to convert the Sultan. You need to realize war was real in those days, too. Despite stories of chivalry, both Crusaders and Mohammedans were brutal. They tortured. They killed each other with burning pitch. Getting through the front lines of one army, across no-man's land, and through the other army was unthinkable in itself. But to get into the presence of the Sultan, and then to try to convert him to Jesus Christ was about as absurd as trying to get to Mao Tse-tung and ask him to register as a member of the Republican Party! But this is exactly what Francis felt led by God to do—and counted on Him to make possible. And sure enough, you know, he carried it off! He didn't succeed in making the con-version—but he did get himself captured, taken into the Sultan's tent, and there—in French—invited Malik Al-Kamil to forsake Islam, to accept the cross, and to turn over Jerusalem to Christian people. History records that the Sultan was fascinated by the little man; that he gave Francis a safe-conduct pass and invited him to visit as long as he wished all the holy places in Palestine. But can you imagine the audacity of this dirty little monk worming his way into the silk tent of the leader of all Islam to speak a word for Jesus?

A later example was a Baptist preacher from the North of England who was born in 1761. He lived in a day when the English speaking world had done very little about extending the outreach of Christianity beyond taking it to immigrants from their own land who were settling in newly discovered parts of the world. But William Carey caught a vision of taking the Gospel of Jesus Christ to the millions of people in India. In February, 1794, he, his wife and one companion arrived in Calcutta to begin the overwhelming project of evangelizing that great sub-continent, and thereby set off the great missionary movement of the 19th and 20th centuries. The motto of his life was, "Expect great things from God; attempt great things for God." He did both. And who would question that he was one of God's special men?

My final example is more controversial, because he is more contemporary. But I have no doubt that history will put Martin Luther King, Jr. among the list of men who have had the audacity to tackle problems that are overwhelming in size and complexity, to demand changes despite resistance as violent as that of Pharaoh, to call on God to act in history, and then to stand back and let men see if He will really come through. I'm sure every time someone has acted in such an audacious way observers have whispered "He's moving to fast. He's speaking in the wrong tone of voice—he should be more conciliatory. He's forgetting about God, and is thinking too much of himself." And without doubt, there have been ego-maniacs who have simply used the name of God for their own ends. But the great changes in the history of the world, the great advances in God's kingdom, seem to have come through those whose daring does border on insolence, whose confidence that they are doing what God wants, makes them disregard personal safety and conventional thought. And I believe Dr. King was such an agent of God in bringing about at least some racial justice in this land which had long been overdue. But he had no idea this was how it would end up when he started out as a pastor fresh out of seminary. I know a Black Methodist minister who lived next door to him in Montgomery, and he told me he had never met a humbler, simpler, more sincere person. When King was thrown into leadership of the bus boycott in Montgomery, he must have quaked and shaked and wondered if he was really right. But he dared to go on, and to attempt the impossible, because he felt this was God's call at this point in history. Toward the end of his life he used to say, "I have a dream." It must have led him for many years, through much trouble.

And what about us? Would anyone, looking on from the outside, call us "audacious men of God"? We do not live in a day of little things—minor problems, small challenges, slow changes. Quite to the contrary, the problems are overwhelming—population explosion, pollution, atomic war, rotting ghettos. The possibilities for good are unequaled—new medicines for sick people; new sources of food for a starving world; mass media by which we can communicate with the here-to-fore unreached. The tempo of change is accelerating with no slow-down in sight. God's need is for men and women and children who will plunge into the middle of all things, and dare to do His will, dare to give Him the opening—dare (if you will) to test Him. The world needs not just *buckets* full of love and courage, but *rivers* flooding all of life, while we sit around measuring out the Gospel in spoonfuls, or even counted drops. I grant you, it will be hard to shift gears. It's contrary to our middle-class, Scotch-Irish, Presbyterian, socially-proper up-bringing. We don't like to go off half-cocked. We don't want to make spectacles of ourselves. We don't want to be called fanatics. We don't want to make anyone mad. We don't want to be made fools of. We don't want to embarrass God.

But I'm struck that God's men, down through the ages, have said "hog wash" to all these fears. Some of them have made mistakes. Some of them have had to eat crow. Some have had to repent of pretty serious sins committed in the name of God. But Jesus said those who have been forgiven a *lot* love more than those who've just had to be forgiven a *little*—so even that isn't fatal. But the one thing common to them all is audacity—to talk *to* God bluntly; to speak *for* God courageously; and to walk *with* God just as far as He would have them go.

Isn't there something really significant that He wants from *you* as an individual, from *us* as a Church? Do you have the *audacity* to tackle it?

Lord Of, or Over, the Nations?

Date: May 14, 1972—Sunday after Ascension

Lectionary: Psalm 2; **Jeremiah 22:1-9**; **Acts 1:1-9**

Hymns: I do not have the bulletin so do not know what hymns
were used.

"Lord, will you at this time restore the kingdom to Israel?...
Thus says the Lord: 'Go down to the house of the king of
Judah, and speak there this word...If you will indeed obey this
word, then there shall enter the gates of this house kings who sit
on the throne of David, riding in chariots and on horses, they, and
their servants, and their people. But if you will not heed these
words, I swear by myself, says the Lord, that this house shall become a desolation.'"

Last Sunday, following the baptism of my young cousin here
at Grace Church, I went to a luncheon at the home of the grand-
mother of the baby. As we were standing around making small talk,
waiting for the meal to be served, I got to ticking off the number of
weddings and funerals and baptisms I had been involved with in
that circle of twenty or so people. For three or four, I am their pastor
as well as their relative. But the rest turn to me only on certain cer-
emonial occasions. And suddenly the thought burst into my mind:
"What does a large family do for a chaplain if it doesn't have some
member who has been ordained?" One of the definitions of chaplain

146

in the dictionary is "a clergyman assigned to the army or navy, or official institutions, or a family or court." In legal circles they often speak of a certain attorney being on "retainer fee" with a particular corporation. That means he's on call in case of an emergency, and ethically he is out of bounds for use by an opponent.

Now there is a constant temptation for us not only to have a lawyer on retainer fee, and a minister relative or friend who will serve as chaplain on state occasions, but to go one step further by trying to build a fence around *God* and attempt to domesticate Him, to make Him our possession, our pet, whom we can expect to come at our beck and call, and to go through His tricks when we give Him the right signal! This yearning crops up in the last question ever put by the disciples to Jesus Christ. We read it this morning in our second lesson—"Lord, will you at this time restore the kingdom to Israel?" You'd think after three years of living with Jesus, and hearing all that He had taught; then after the searing experience of the crucifixion, and the transforming one of the resurrection, they would have been set free of such petty thoughts. But here, forty days after Easter, they are still wanting to know, "When are we going to get our goodies, so that the world will at last know for sure that *we're* Your favored ones?"

I guess it was inevitable that such possessiveness should set in. God had become one of them to break through the hardness of their hearts, to show them what He was like, and the nature of His love. But just as some of the most powerfully healing drugs have bad side-effects, so His identification with men in one time, one place, and one nation, encouraged them to draw as a final deduction the idea "Then He *belongs* to us. And all the benefits He brings will come *our* way!" So Jesus had to do one last thing, to "stomp" on this dangerous idea before it could spread any further. In St. Luke's dramatic way, he presents the Lord as saying "You shall be my witnesses in Jerusalem and in all Judea and Samaria and to the end of the earth," and then he adds "And when he had said this, as they were looking on, he was lifted up, and a cloud took him out of their sight" We refer to this every Sunday we say the

147

Apostles' Creed, when we come to that section "the third day He rose again from the dead, he ascended into heaven and sitteth on the right hand of God the Father Almighty..." Only a lot of us miss the point, and think that the primary issue is the disposition, or location, of Jesus' body. In my opinion, that really doesn't matter in the least. What is vital is that we realize the way God had identified Himself in a unique way for some thirty years in Jesus of Nazareth with a *particular* time and place and religious group has now come to an end. The disciples are sent out as witnesses to the "end of the earth," for God is—as He always has been—Lord of *all* nations and races and peoples. Jesus was a "for instance" in His eternal Word for mankind. The Ascension was God's way of tearing down any fence the disciples might have wanted to build around His Son to establish a claim that he was *theirs* in any exclusive sense. The people who included in the Creed the phrase "sitteth at the right hand of God the Father Almighty" had grown up familiar with a saying that "the right hand of God is everywhere." Jesus Christ's liberation from any limits of time or space or culture is what we are celebrating in the Ascension.

But God's presence everywhere, and love for everyone, were not radically new concepts to those who had grown up in the Jewish tradition. They might have been forgotten, but a similar, if not identical, message had come from God through the prophet Jeremiah some six hundred years before. We read an excerpt from his life story this morning, in our First Lesson. He was a prophet in Jerusalem before and after the year 600 B.C. It was a time of great turmoil and upheaval, both within Judah and internationally. There was great social corruption, and the various kings were playing what we today would call "Russian roulette" in their diplomacy and military alliances. Egypt and Assyria and Babylon were battling back and forth across the ancient world seeking for supremacy, and Judah was treated as a pawn on a giant chessboard. But the religious leaders in the Temple kept telling the king, "It's all right. God is the God of Zion. As long as the Temple, His house, is here, nothing will happen to Jerusalem. God will protect *us*, for we are *His*."

They didn't say, but it is clearly implied, "and He is *ours!*" They figured they had God on a "retainer fee." He was their "chaplain," their pet puppy who would always roll over whenever they "scratched His stomach," so to speak, by sacrificing an animal or saying the proper religious words.

Then the word of the Lord came to Jeremiah, "Go down to the king's house and tell him that's not the way it is at all. I have made an agreement, a covenant, with your people. So long as they fulfill their obligations, I will uphold them as a kingdom. But when they lie and steal and kill, they have broken the covenant, and my commitment to them is no longer valid. In fact, I make a solemn vow that the house of David will become desolate, and Jerusalem will be wiped out as a city." Now that is quite a message for Jeremiah, just an ordinary priest, to have to deliver face-to-face to the King. However, he said it, not just to one king but to four or five in a row, as they sat on the throne. And he said it in the Temple in a sermon. And he said it out on the street. For the people of Judah in proclaiming that Yahweh was "the Lord of our nation" had gradually come to think of this as meaning "the Lord who *belongs* to our nation" rather than "the Lord who *rules over* us." So God sent word they were badly mistaken. He said, I am not fenced in. I am not owned by you. I am the Lord of other nations as well. Nebuchadnezzar, king of Babylon, is my servant too. He does not *know* me, as you do, but he is mine. I have blessed him, and I can use him for my glory. I do not have the special relationship with him I have had with you in Judah, but if you break the covenant between us, I shall not hesitate to use Nebuchadnezzar to punish you and humble you and bring you to your senses. For I am the Lord *over* your nation, not a Lord *owned by* it."

Now the words of Jeremiah, when I read or hear them, send a shiver down my spine. For they come through to me not as dusty phrases from some sermon preached twenty-six hundred years ago, but the Word of God more up-to-date than this morning's headlines. For once again I fear a people—this time the American people—have fallen into the same error which made the disciples ask

Jesus when he was going to restore the kingdom to "our kind of folks," or the leaders of Jerusalem dismiss Jeremiah as a fanatic because everybody knew God was on the side of the city which contained His Temple. Just as they had slipped into defining "Lord of the nation" as "Lord *belonging to*" rather than "*Lord over*" it, so have many in America. And perhaps this is even more common among some of our leaders than among the rank and file of us. But the fact we think we have God on a "retainer fee," that he is hired to be our chaplain, does not mean he is. He is our Lord—in the sense of being Lord over us. But he is also Lord of China and Russia and both Vietnams; and He can use them as His servants, just as he used Nebuchadnezzar of Babylon. He even used Nebuchadnezzar against Judah, when these His special people, violated their agreement with Him by lying and stealing and shedding innocent blood.

Do you see why a study of Jeremiah discomforts me? The parallels are too close for comfort. For some years now I have been very ill at ease regarding our nation's stand in Southeast Asia, yet I have had relatively little to say about it, for while I felt what we were doing was wrong, I had no alternative to suggest, and it seems irresponsible to condemn one line of action unless I'm prepared to offer a substitute. But I was blasted off dead center this past Monday night. When I heard the news that President Nixon had announced the mining of the harbors of North Vietnam I almost became physically ill. And there has been a burning in my bones ever since. At long last I must speak out. I realize I may be wrong, and may be dumping on you just my personal convictions on war and peace. If that should be the case, I ask your pardon, for I have no right to afflict you in a sermon with my political judgment. But I believe this is something much deeper moving in me this week. I feel it is the word of God and if it is, woe unto me if I do not speak it to you, whether you like it or not.

As I look at our nation, I see a society which is violating the moral laws and ethical foundations of the covenant God makes with His people. God hates a lie. And deception has become so much a part of our government's way of doing business that officials

150

are no longer even embarrassed when they are found out. The President tells us one thing, the Secretary of State another, and the Secretary of Defense a third. And who know where the truth is to be found? The Lord who rules over nations commanded, "You shall not bear false witness."

And God hates a double standard. It was common practice in the ancient world to treat justly one's near-neighbors, and others strong enough to hit back—but it was considered all right to deal with aliens and widows and orphans any way you wanted to. Yet Yahweh said He would not tolerate two levels of ethics. In the Ten Commandments, protection of the Sabbath must be the same for the "manservant and maidservant and sojourner that is within your gates" as it was for the head of the clan. And exploitation of the helpless was one of the charges made by Jeremiah against the King of Judah. Yet our national policy has become one of a double standard in regard to moral responsibility on war. We, as a nation, in the Nuremberg Trials at the end of World War II charged leaders of Germany as being guilty of crimes committed during the Nazi regime. When they protested they were merely carrying out orders, we said that was no excuse. And this policy was confirmed in the My Lai case when Lt. Calley was found guilty of murder. Yet we turn right around and deny to young men the right of selective conscientious objection when they say they might fight in some war, but find what we are doing in Southeast Asia at this time to be a violation of what they consider right. Now whether we were wise at Nuremberg, I am not sure. But we cannot have our cake and eat it too. We cannot make individuals morally responsible for their behavior in war, and then deny them the right to exercise that responsibility when it comes to the draft. There is something sick about a nation that ties to straddle the fence in this way.

And there is something morally sick about a nation which has such awesome power, and throws that power about as recklessly as a poker player who ups the ante on a hand by two more blue chips—especially when the stakes involve far more suffering and death on the part of others than we experience. We in America are distressed, and rightly so, by our casualties and prisoners of war. But in the sight of God the death of a Vietnamese—from the South or North—is as costly as that of an American. A report came out this week in the *Scientific American* that the explosives we unloaded in *South* Vietnam between 1965 and 1971 equaled the destruction in 363 atomic bombs of the size dropped on Hiroshima. Earlier it was said all this was done to protect the South Vietnamese people—though we all catch the irony of the communiqué which reported that a small village had been totally destroyed in order to "save" it. I have been increasingly skeptical about how much the little people of South Vietnam—as distinct from government leaders—want to be "saved" by us at such a price. Yet I have held my tongue, realizing a Communist take-over would also mean a bloody purge. But this week our President has finally said what many suspected, that the motive behind this latest escalation is that he does not intend to be the first President of the United States to lose a war. It has become, or is at last admitted to be, a matter of pride, or prestige, or face-saving. Yet if I read the Bible correctly, God has no patience with this kind of pride—in an individual, or a church, or a nation. We are not called to hold our heads up high, but "to walk humbly with our God." The nation which is just will get from others all the esteem it needs or can use. The nation which is primarily concerned with bolstering its own reputation among others, is riding for a fall. God's prophets have warned of this down through the centuries, and history has proved that God will not be mocked.

There are many other specifics to which I could point, if time permitted. But these are sufficient to tell you why I have felt a burning in my bones this past week which will not permit me to remain silent any longer. There is a sickness of soul in our nation. There is a violation of the moral obligations which make up our end of the covenant relationship with God. If we continue in our present course, we are inviting upon ourselves His judgment and wrath. I cannot tell you in what form it will come, but that it will come I am sure. The kings of Judah and the leaders in the Temple were convinced it could never happen to them. They said "Yahweh is the Lord of our nation" and by that they meant He *belongs* to our nation." But what God means by "Lord of the nation" is Ruler *over* it"—over America, and China and Russia and every other land. He is a God who wants peace and justice in His kingdom. And he will have them. Any nation which refuses to devote itself to His purposes, and seeks instead its own ends, will be rebuked, and if need be, destroyed. Do not delude yourself into thinking that we have God on a retainer fee, that He is our chaplain or mascot. He is our Lord, our Ruler, our King. When the disciples showed they believed Jesus somehow belonged especially to them, He ascended into heaven, to show He was free, and Lord of all nations in an equal manner. Though it may hurt our national pride to find we are just one among many, let us rejoice that is so, for no other kind of God would be worthy of our praise.

WHOSE TEMPLE ARE YOU?

Date: September 16, 1973—14th Sunday after Pentecost, 12th
    anniversary of organization of Grace Church

Lectionary: Psalm 84; **Joshua 2:1-3a, 13-24;**
    I Corinthians 3:1-11, 16-17

Hymns: I do not have a copy of the bulletin so do not know what
    hymns were used.

*This sermon was preached the Sunday after I announced my resignation
as pastor of Grace Church in order to accept a call as staff associate with
the General Executive Board of the Presbyterian Church, U.S. in Atlanta.*

There's a book out now—some of you have read it—by Eric Berne
called *What Do You Say After You've Said Hello?* I'm glad he wrote
it, and someday I hope to have a chance to read it. But that wasn't
the one I was looking for yesterday. I wished desperately someone had
published a volume entitled *What Do You Say After You've Said
Goodbye?* For what shall I say to you when the Sunday after my resignation was announced coincides with the completion of twelve full
years of life as an organized congregation for Grace Church?

Let me begin on a very personal note, and then move to
something more Biblical. Some of you have asked me why I want
you to concur with me in requesting Presbytery to dissolve the pastoral relationship between us. There are a variety of reasons. I'll
not try to deal with them all. But I have grown weary. Maybe it's

just old age coming on, but I find that I don't have quite the same zest and drive I used to in providing you with leadership. I suspect much of it comes from repetition. The turn-over in membership, the coming and going of interns, have charged my batteries many times over. But twelve and a half years is a long time, especially when that was preceded by six and a half years in Crossett where my approach was quite similar. Under normal circumstances at such a midpoint in a minister's career—you know, I've been ordained twenty years now and can anticipate twenty more of professional life—I might have desired, and received and accepted a call to another church. But it has become apparent that divorced men, unless they are remarried, rarely receive calls as pastors. Frankly, I don't think my divorce has been a hindrance to my ministry here—rather a help in many cases—but this fact seems to blow the minds of pulpit nominating committees. So I began thinking of other alternatives, lest I get in a rut here to your hurt and mine. I got professional help in assessing my skills and interests. I was not surprised when it was suggested that I consider some type of administrative position, so long as it involved lots of contact with people, and problem solving and organizing. I very much wanted to stay in the structure of the organized church, so when our denomination sent out word of some openings which almost matched my profile I perked up. I didn't quite fit in a couple of them but then came a third which almost seemed to have my name written on the job description. The people in Atlanta agreed and asked me to fill it. I had that "aha" feeling. There was almost a snap, as when two matched parts of a piece of machinery fit together. This is often the underside, the human viewpoint, of a divine call. It is not easy to pull up roots after living this long with you; it is not easy to leave my family. But I believe I am doing what is right for me—because I think this is what God wants for me at this point in my life. What happens afterward, I do not know. But this step I should take at this time.

However, my concern is not *solely* for myself. It may not be purely coincidence that we talk today of *my* leaving as *you* complete your twelfth year of life as a church. In Biblical times when a boy had his twelfth birthday he came of age. I feel you as a congregation have also reached a level of maturity which calls for some basic changes in behavior patterns, perhaps a shift in direction. We would be worried if an adolescent continued to act exactly the way he did when he was a child. I doubt you would have done the honest soul-searching which you will be forced to do now, if I had remained. I wonder if you would not have hesitated to reject some of our familiar ways for new ones, out of respect for me. The motive—love—is excellent, and I am grateful; but the outcome could be harmful. Then there are some individuals in this congregation to whom I have never been able to minister, really. This does not mean either they or I should be blamed. We just operate on different wave lengths. But these folk have a right to have their needs met, too. Perhaps someone else can do it. It's their turn now. And what about those of you who say, and show, that I have meant a great deal to you? It's for your sake too—maybe for you most of all—that I should go.

To help you understand that, let me recall for you the passage from Joshua which we read as our first lesson this morning. It's most appropriate for the Sunday when Grace Church "comes of age." Joshua was the leader who took over from Moses when the children of Israel, having completed their time in the wilderness, reached the border of the Promised Land. It was Joshua who led them across the River Jordan, showed them how to capture Jericho, and then supervised their conquest and settlement of Canaan. Now Joshua is growing old. So he calls together the elders and leaders of all twelve tribes, shares with them a concern, and challenges them for the future. Having rehearsed the goodness of God in looking after them through the years and providing for their every need, he then points out their tendency to try to hang on to both the living Lord of the present, Yahweh, and the gods of the past, those worshipped by their forefathers before Abraham. He warned them it was impossible to have both. In this decision, it was either/or, not both/and. He gave them freedom to make their choice-yet he did set an example. He said he and his house would serve the Lord. The people were caught up in enthusiasm and echoed "Yeah, that's what we want to do!" But Joshua, being a faithful leader, would not let them rush headlong into such a decision. He warned them of the cost. Yahweh will not tolerate a fence-straddler. If they throw their lot with Him they must go the whole way. It's all or nothing. But the people were determined. They had caught a vision of what life with Yahweh would be like, and they made a covenant. "The Lord our God we will serve, and his voice we will obey." And from that point they moved ahead into a new stage of their development and mission.

Now I want you to jump ahead some twelve to fifteen hundred years. Instead of Canaan where the tribes of Israel have recently come, we are in Corinth, a city in Greece where the Christian Church has recently appeared. Instead of Joshua, the leader is Paul. Instead of foreign gods worshipped long ago by forefathers, the people's love for God is being split and deflected by their loyalty to certain human beings. There had been various leaders in the church at Corinth, including Paul himself. The other outstanding one was a man named Apollos, who came from Alexandria down in Egypt. He, apparently, was a brilliant preacher. But instead of rejoicing in their varied gifts, and benefitting from each, the people polarized. Some rallied around one and some around the other, and parties developed within the church. "… one says, 'I belong to Paul,' and another 'I belong to Apollos.'" Then the writer asks, and answers, a question. "What then is Apollos? What is Paul? Servants through whom you believed, as the Lord assigned to each. I planted, Apollos watered, but God gave the growth. So neither he who plants nor he who waters is anything, but only God who gives the growth."

How tragic it is when men who have been sent as means to an end become the goal itself, the focal point around which all turns. This is the stuff out of which idolatry is made. Neither Paul nor Apollos wanted it to happen, yet it did. So easily can we make servants of God into idols around which our religion revolves. Just yesterday I heard of a woman who has been looking in vain for twenty years for a church where she could be happy because she had one very outstanding pastor in her youth, and she will not be content until she can find somebody just like him. That is looking back, at the gods of the fathers instead of living in the present with the Lord God. That is looking down at a bit of creation and worshipping it instead of looking up at the Creator Himself. It has happened over and over again in history. Whenever a leader is the agent through whom people catch a vision of God, by means of whom they are excited and make a commitment, there is a danger that some of those people are going to take their eye off God and focus on the leader. Every minister can be so misused. The longer one stays, the greater the temptation. And when one has founded a church and been its only pastor, the chances grow still more. It may sound presumptuous on my part to sound a warning, but I would rather risk the label of "arrogant" than be derelict in my duty. If there has ever been any doubt in your mind, this is not *my* church, nor is my personality what holds it together. If that were the only cement we had, then we might as well fall apart right now. I don't think I have become indispensable to this church, nor to the religious life of anyone in it. I am leaving before anyone makes the tragic mistake of putting me in the center. And let me plead with you right now not to feel your love for me requires you to oppose my successor. He, or she, will simply be another servant of God. There is no room, there is not time or energy, for friction between those who say "I am of Paul" or "I am of Apollos."

Instead, there is great benefit to be derived from a succession of leaders. The apostle wrote, "I planted, Apollos watered." Paul had been the one who came to Corinth, a tough seaport, and started the church from scratch. Apollos followed some time later, and apparently built up a much larger congregation through his preaching. But there was no competition for honor between them. They complemented each other—one filling out what the other lacked. The Holy Spirit has a whole variety of gifts to bestow, but no one individual can receive them all. Some are organizers, some eloquent speakers, some masters of prayer; some are great with youth, others with older folk. One of the reasons I am leaving Grace Church is my awareness that while I am very strong in certain areas, I am just as weak in others. If you are going to be mature, you need to be well-rounded, filled out. By calling someone with different gifts, you can grow in new areas.

The greatest thing which can happen to you through my leaving is a re-discovery of Who the center of this church really is. What is the foundation on which all else is built? "Like a skilled master builder I laid a foundation, and another man (will soon be) building upon it…(But) no other foundation can anyone lay than that which is laid, which is Jesus Christ." I hope I can say that of Grace Church as honestly as Paul did of the Corinthian one. He is the One through whom we have come to know what God is like. Through Him we have learned what God would have us do. He is the yardstick by which all our decisions are measured. He feeds us and gives us strength. He will remain long after I am gone. To use slightly different terms, but saying the same thing, "God's Spirit dwells in you"—Grace Church. And if He is here, what more could you want? Of course we shall be sad when we cease to see each other weekly as we have these past years. But have no fear about the future of Grace Church. If I have done my work well, and if you have grown in the faith as I believe you have, you are built on a solid foundation—that of Jesus Christ. "You are God's temple and…God's Spirit dwells in you." Love Him, obey Him, make Him your center and your Lord—and a whole glorious future awaits you. I leave, not for lack of love for you, to make way for new growth as you "come of age."

CPSIA information can be obtained
at www.ICGtesting.com
Printed in the USA
FFOW04n2216200317
33586FF